W9-CPN-561

CULTURE LOVERS

& Other
Artsy Types

VGM Careers for You Series

CAREERS
FOR
CULTURE
LOVERS
& Other
Artsy Types

Marjorie Eberts
Margaret Gisler

Second Edition

VGM Career Horizons
NTC/Contemporary Publishing Group

Library of Congress Cataloging-in-Publication Data

Eberts, Marjorie.
    Careers for culture lovers & other artsy types / Marjorie
Eberts and Margaret Gisler. — 2nd ed.
       p.   cm. — (VGM careers for you series)
    ISBN 0-8442-1966-5 (cloth). — ISBN 0-8442-1976-2 (pbk.)
    1. Arts—Vocational guidance—United States. I. Gisler,
Margaret. II. Title. III. Title: Careers for culture lovers and
other artsy types. IV. Series.
NX503.E24 1999
700'.23'73—dc21
                                     98–54273
                                         CIP

To Anthony Poon, a very
talented architect and
musician. You are
a true culture lover who
appreciates the arts.

Published by VGM Career Horizons
A division of NTC/Contemporary Publishing Group, Inc.
4255 West Touhy Avenue, Lincolnwood (Chicago), Illinois 60646-1975 U.S.A.
Copyright © 1999 by NTC/Contemporary Publishing Group, Inc.
Printed in the United States of America
International Standard Book Number: 0-8442-1966-5 (cloth)
                                         0-8442-1976-2 (paper)
99 00 01 02 03 04 MV 18 17 16 15 14 13 12 11 10 9 8 7 6 5 4 3 2 1

Contents

Foreword

Art has the power to educate, entertain, and inspire us. Cultural events are a welcome respite from our daily routines, a chance to appreciate the creativity of others, to contemplate new ideas, to reevaluate our own perspectives on life. The fine arts offer more than recreation. They enhance the quality of our lives and contribute to our overall well-being.

For culture lovers, there's no greater pleasure than listening to a favorite symphony, going to the opera or ballet, or spending an afternoon admiring the work of a new painter. If you value the fine arts, you may also dream of finding a way to turn your avocation into a career.

Careers for Culture Lovers explores dozens of jobs behind the scenes in the fine arts. Music teachers, museum curators, choreographers, and set designers explain how they got started and describe the joys and frustrations of their jobs. They discuss the day-to-day work that keeps symphonies, theater companies, and art galleries in existence and allows the public to share the visions of talented composers, playwrights, and visual artists.

Culture lovers have a unique opportunity to provide that link between artist and audience. Through their work, teachers and arts administrators inspire future artists and create future audiences. Whatever their job descriptions, culture lovers use their skills in countless ways to cultivate in others the same appreciation for the arts that enriches their own lives.

The Editors of VGM

CHAPTER ONE

Careers for Culture Lovers
Enjoying the Arts While You Work

"Fine art is that in which the hand, the head, and the heart of man go together." JOHN RUSKIN, *The Two Paths*

Some experiences are very special to culture lovers. They savor time spent in art museums appreciating the creations of artists from Leonardo Da Vinci to pop artist Andy Warhol. They relish the opportunity to view the arabesques and pirouettes of dancers as a story unfolds in a ballet. They feel themselves transformed as they listen to the music of a symphony orchestra performing a work by Beethoven, Tchaikovsky, or Mozart. They lean forward eagerly to view the stage when the curtain goes up for a play. It's not just art, dance, music, and the theater that gives a great satisfaction to culture lovers; they enjoy viewing the amazing pictures of outstanding photographers, the imaginative buildings of world-renowned architects, and the magnificent jewelry of skilled artisans. Each work of art presents something special to the senses of culture lovers, whether it is the music they hear or the sculpture they view.

The magnetic pull of culture dominates the lives of culture lovers. They spend their money on paintings, prints, sculpture, tapes, CDs, and tickets to ballets, concerts, and theatrical productions. And the homes of culture lovers reflect their overwhelming interest in the arts, with music constantly filling the air, rooms decorated with works of art, and magazines and books on the different arts sitting on coffee and bedside tables.

Many culture lovers are not content to stand on the sidelines when it comes to enjoying the arts. They find time to be artists,

1

musicians, singers, dancers, and actors. For some arts lovers, this means a part-time job, while for others it is a favorite avocation or recreation. Art lovers spend hours of free time painting, sculpting, and making mosaics. Music lovers play in bands, orchestras, and chamber groups in their communities; sing in choral groups; or perform with the local opera company. And both singers and dancers often enjoy starring in musical productions, while actors put on makeup to do plays.

A Quick Look at Careers for Culture Lovers

Career opportunities as artists, musicians, singers, dancers, and actors are extremely limited. Successful careers in these areas require both talent and dedication. Few individuals can reach the stratospheric heights of international acclaim in the arts that Picasso, Pablo Casals, Beverly Sills, Jessica Tandy, Laurence Olivier, and Mikhail Baryshnikov attained. Furthermore, competition is so keen in the arts that only a few are able to earn a living entirely from their artistic endeavors. Fortunately, there's an amazing variety of jobs for culture lovers who wish to spend their work hours in jobs closely aligned to their own personal interests.

This book is dedicated to helping all culture lovers find jobs that will let them work in areas that they value so highly. Here is a bird's-eye view of some of the careers that you will read about in this book.

Careers for Art Lovers

Wherever art is displayed, there are usually jobs that will appeal to art lovers. Museums are especially appealing workplaces with their collections of paintings, sculpture, and other art forms.

And depending on their size, museums need directors, curators, administrators, fund-raisers, financial managers, educators, gift shop employees, and guards. A job in an art gallery lets art lovers be part of the exciting world of buying and selling art. Jobs for art lovers are certainly not limited to museums and art galleries. Being an art critic for a newspaper or magazine allows art lovers to spend their days viewing and writing about art. Restorers and framers have hands-on jobs that actually let them handle art. And many jobs exist in public and private schools for those who wish to help people of all ages acquire skills in painting, drawing, sculpting, and other art forms.

Careers for Music Lovers

Music lovers with considerable expertise in music will find the greatest number of jobs associated with music as teachers. Teaching presents an opportunity to help fledgling musicians acquire basic skills and expert musicians refine their skills. Besides teaching, skilled musicians can find very satisfying jobs as music therapists helping people in hospitals, mental health facilities, and nursing homes improve their health through music. Music lovers don't have to be skilled musicians, however, to find a wide variety of jobs with symphony orchestras, opera companies, choirs, and theatrical production companies. The larger a musical group is, the greater the number of people required to handle administrative functions and backstage activities. Knowledgeable music lovers who like to write can find jobs as critics with newspapers and magazines, while those with technical skills can find jobs in the recording industry creating tapes, CDs, and videos. And of course, there are jobs selling and repairing musical instruments as well as glamour jobs working with musical artists from Madonna to Billy Joel. Music lovers can even spend all their time with music as disc jockeys.

Careers for Dance Lovers

From ballroom dancing to viewing ballet and folk dance companies, dance is more popular than ever before, giving dance lovers many job opportunities. Dance companies offer many jobs to dance lovers who wish to help dancers prepare for and present performances. Behind every dance performance, there are choreographers, costume designers, wardrobe handlers, and stagehands. Dance lovers will also find some special jobs with dance companies, for example, movement notators, who record as many details as are necessary to restage a dance performance. There are also reconstructors, who take these details and train the dance company to perform the dance according to the notations, and autographers, who put the notations in a form that can be distributed to all the dancers. A love of dance can also lead to a career as a dance therapist, restoring people to health through movement. Through teaching, dance lovers can share their love of dance with others. Both children and adults are eager to learn ballet, modern dance, folk dancing, and social dancing.

Careers for Theater Lovers

There's no business like show business, from Broadway productions to local dinner theaters. Wherever the lights go down and the curtains go up, there are jobs for theater lovers. For most theatrical productions, there are far more people working behind the scenes than the audience sees on the stage. For all these productions, writers, directors, producers, publicists, business support staff, costume designers, dressers, set designers, hair stylists, prompters, sound and light engineers, and stagehands are required. Unfortunately, most theater jobs, except those of an administrative or clerical nature, end with the final curtain of a production. Only jobs with League of Resident Theaters (LORT) are year-round jobs. Most theater lovers are freelancers who move from one show to another.

More Careers for Culture Lovers

Literature, photography, interior design, architecture, furniture, textiles, and jewelry can also be included within the broad world of fine arts. The creators of these aesthetically pleasing art forms require many assistants to produce and sell their finished works. Culture lovers interested in these arts can find jobs in museums, galleries, and stores. For example, working in an antique store can be a wonderful opportunity to be surrounded by beautiful and historical objects.

A vast amount of money is distributed each year by governmental bodies, corporations, individuals, and foundations that support the arts. Decisions have to be made about which arts groups will receive this money. Culture lovers can find a variety of challenging jobs in the organizations that disburse these funds.

Dream Jobs for Culture Lovers

When culture lovers read want ads in newspapers or magazines or look for positions on the Internet, they are always searching for jobs that will allow them to spend more time working in areas that are closely tied to their interests. The following position descriptions would surely capture the attention of many arts lovers.

DANCE THERAPIST   Full-time position with prestigious long-term care facility. Competitive pay and benefits.

MUSIC EDUCATOR   Private school seeks teachers for child groups, birth to age seven. Must sing on pitch, follow rhythm. Will train the rest. Flexible hours and excellent pay.

SENIOR ASSOCIATE DIRECTOR   Local university seeks individual to assist the director of development in the design, implementation, and management of a program of activities to generate philanthropic gift support to the Museum of Art. Specific responsibility for segments of major gift prospect research, cultivation, solicitation, and stewardship activities required for the anticipated capital campaign. Bachelor's degree required, as is at least four years experience.

LAYOUT AND PASTEUP PERSON A publisher of rare and first edition books is seeking an individual familiar with Macintosh system and two-color layout/design technique. This person must be experienced and able to work with editors in creating sophisticated artwork.

FULL-TIME SALES REPRESENTATIVE Here is an exciting opportunity to join a world-renowned international retailer of exquisite jewelry and fine merchandise. Our Boston location is currently interviewing for sales professionals. Qualified applicants must be friendly, diligent individuals with a high degree of enthusiasm and professionalism. Candidates must have one year of related experience.

Job Qualifications

Culture lovers appreciate objects and experiences that arouse their senses. A love of culture, while essential, is not sufficient qualification for obtaining many jobs in the arts. Specialized training or academic degrees are required for many of these jobs. For example, culture lovers wanting to help people through music or dance therapy must combine college courses in music with extensive work in the behavioral and biological sciences. Quite often in the arts arena, a master's degree is a prerequisite for even being considered for a position. And there are many jobs where holding a double master's degree or a doctorate is necessary to obtain a specific job. Fortunately, a considerable part of the course work allows most culture lovers to gain more and more knowledge of their favorite art forms. And culture lovers seeking careers associated with the arts realize that they must have the best training and education in order to meet the challenges that lie ahead in their careers.

Starting Your Career

Because working closely with art, music, dance, theater, and other fine arts is so immensely satisfying to culture lovers, there is considerable competition for many entry-level positions. Jobs in museums and with symphony orchestras and theatrical groups are especially competitive. Besides requiring the appropriate educational background, entry-level jobs typically go to those with some experience. The best way to garner this experience is by working as a volunteer or intern, which allows you to explore a career in a specific art as well as network with individuals who may know about job openings.

Culture lovers can find out about positions in the arts through looking at advertisements in newspapers and magazines associated with the different arts. In addition, many jobs can be found by using the job search capabilities of the Internet. If you would like a job with a particular organization such as a symphony orchestra or a foundation, you should explore the organization's Web site as many have job listings.

Where the Jobs Are

For many culture lovers, relocation is the name of the game when they are looking for employment in the arts, since the largest number and variety of jobs are found in the major metropolitan areas. Nevertheless, it is not essential for culture lovers to seek employment in just a few large cities. Scattered across the country in communities of every size there are jobs for arts lovers. For example, jobs in education will be found in even the smallest towns where culture lovers can teach in schools or give lessons in their homes.

For Further Reading

A deeper appreciation of the arts emerges as people learn more about them. There are many excellent guides that will help you become better acquainted with the different arts.

Art

Baigell, Matthew. *A Concise History of Painting and Sculpture*. Boulder, CO: Westview Press, 1996.

Cole, Bruce, and Adeiheid Gealt. *Art of the Western World: From Ancient Greece to Post-Modernism*. New York: Touchstone Books, 1991.

Fleming, William. *Arts and Ideas*. San Diego, CA: Harcourt Brace & Company, 1997.

Gombrich, E. H. *The Story of Art*. New York: Phaidon Press Inc., 1995.

Tansey, Richard, et al. *Gardner's Art Through the Ages*. San Diego, California: Harcourt Brace & Company, 1995.

Music

Haas, Karl. *Inside Music: How to Understand, Listen To, and Enjoy Good Music*. Garden City, NY: Anchor Books, 1991.

Stanley, John. *Classical Music: An Introduction to Classical Music Through the Great Composers and Their Masterworks*. Pleasantville, NY: Readers Digest, 1997.

Steinberg, Michael. *The Symphony: A Listener's Guide*. New York: Oxford University Press, 1995.

Waugh, Alexander. *Opera: A New Way of Listening*. New York: Stewart, Tabori and Chang, 1996.

Dance

Adshead, Janet, and June Layson, editors. *Dance History: An Introduction*. London: Routledge, 1994.

Balanchine, George, and Francis Mason. *101 Stories of the Great Ballets*. New York: Anchor Books, 1989.

Brenner, Summer. *Dancers and the Dance: Stories*. Minneapolis, MN: Coffeehouse Press, 1990.

Brown, Jean Morrison, and Charles H. Wood Ford, editors. *The Vision of Modern Dance: In the Words of Its Creators*. Princeton, NJ: Princeton Book Company, Publishers, 1998.

Theater

Allison, Alexander W., Arthur C. Carr, and Arthur M. Eastman. *Masterpieces of the Drama*. New York: Prentice Hall Press, 1991.

Bordman, Gerald Martin. *The Oxford Companion to American Theater*. New York: Oxford University Press, 1992.

Brockett, Oscar Gross. *The Essential Theater*. San Diego, CA: Harcourt Brace & Company, 1998.

Hartnoll, Phyllis, and Enoch Brater. *The Theater: A Concise History (World of Art)*. London: Thames & Hudson, Inc., 1998.

CHAPTER TWO

Careers for Art Lovers

Enjoying Painting, Sculpture, and Other Art Forms

"Art is not a handicraft, it is the transmission of feeling the artist has experienced." LEO TOLSTOY, *Tr. Maude*

P eople who love art can lose themselves in a painting, sculpture, mosaic, mural, or drawing. Not only do they appreciate seeing the works of well-known artists, they also enjoy seeing the efforts of those just beginning to exercise their talents. A deep satisfaction can be found in art. It is something to be studied for pleasure or to learn how the artist felt about subjects such as religion, family, and social justice.

Fortunately for art lovers, the enjoyment of art does not have to be a leisure time activity; there are many jobs that will let them spend their workdays surrounded by art. They can have extremely satisfying careers working in art museums or galleries. Jobs with newspapers and magazines as art commentators or critics give art lovers a chance to share their opinions of works of art with others. Art lovers also have the opportunity to educate both children and adults on artistic techniques and the history of art as teachers. In fact, wherever there is art, a variety of jobs exist for those who wish to work in some way with art.

Art Museums—Paradise for Art Lovers

According to the American Association of Museums (AAM), a museum is an organized and permanent nonprofit institution, essentially educational or aesthetic in purpose, with professional staff, that owns and uses tangible objects, cares for them, and exhibits them to the public on some regular schedule. While this is an all-purpose definition of museum, the word *art* in art museum indicates that these museums care for and exhibit works of art. The focus of art museums varies greatly. An art museum may show works of art from ancient times to the present in many mediums, as the Metropolitan Museum of Art in New York City and the Art Institute of Chicago do. Or an art museum may specialize in the art of one period, artist, or medium. For example, the Museum of Modern Art in New York City is devoted to the collection and exhibition of modern art; the Asian Art Museum of San Francisco concentrates on Asian art from many eras. No matter what specialty interests an art lover, there is probably an art museum devoted to that interest. It is possible for art lovers to find jobs at museums devoted solely to craft and folk art, Native American, or French Impressionist collections. By reading the *Official Museum Directory* published annually, art lovers can find out just about everything they need to know about individual museums. The directory has information about museum personnel; areas of collections; and the nature, size, and scope of each of the facilities listed.

The Louvre, founded in 1793, is generally considered the first real art museum. In the United States, it was not until the end of the 1800s that the number of art museums began to grow rapidly. Today, art lovers will find major art museums in large cities like New York, Boston, Minneapolis, San Francisco, Los Angeles, Chicago, and Philadelphia. They can also find art museums scattered across the country in towns as diverse as Helena, Montana; Akron, Ohio; Utica, New York; Anchorage, Alaska; Andover, Massachusetts; and Sarasota, Florida.

How Museums Work

The purpose of museums is to collect, preserve, research, exhibit, and interpret objects of lasting value for the public, according to the AAM. Museums obtain their collections by buying, trading with other museums, and receiving gifts. The museum staff keeps an accurate record of every object in the museum. The staff repairs and restores damaged objects and employs scientific techniques to protect the collection from deterioration. Most museums store the greater part of their collections for scholarly investigation and only exhibit their choicest objects for their patrons. Museums also offer a wide variety of educational activities, including courses, lectures, publications, and guide services.

Career Options in Art Museums

Staff members are needed for a wide variety of positions in art museums—from designing exhibits, soliciting funds, and guarding collections to conducting research, keeping financial records, and sweeping the floors. In large museums, staff members often have duties in a finely defined area, such as curator of Egyptian art. However, in small museums, employees need to be "jacks-of-all-trades," capable of handling diverse tasks from training docents to cataloging objects. In all art museums, there is a need for people with sound business backgrounds to run the financial side of the organization. Employees are also needed to handle the clerical and maintenance tasks.

Because art museums are so very different in size, budgets, and collections, the following job descriptions of key personnel give just the basic functions of each position.

DIRECTOR   carries out the policy of the board of the museum and is the manager of all functions of the museum. All staff positions report to the director.

CURATOR   is responsible for the care and interpretation of all objects in the museum and for research on the collections. The curator recommends acquisitions and removals of artworks from the collection. Duties may include organizing exhibitions.

CONSERVATOR   scientifically analyzes museum objects to prevent deterioration and repairs them when necessary. The conservator is responsible for keeping objects in the collection at the proper temperature and humidity and protected from pests, pollution, and harmful light exposure.

EXHIBITS DESIGNER   turns the ideas of the museum's curators and educators into drawings or scale models for permanent, temporary, or traveling exhibits. The designer may also be responsible for setting up the exhibit.

REGISTRAR   is in charge of cataloging objects in the collection and maintaining proper documents such as insurance and the copyright and reproduction rights for them. Responsibilities also include the packing, unpacking, shipping, and storing of art objects plus the handling of customs problems.

EDUCATOR   develops, implements, and supervises the formal and informal teaching programs of the museum with the goal of increasing the public's understanding of the art collection. Duties can include in-service instruction for docents, workshops for museum faculty, and the setting up of lecture series, film programs, tours, special events, seminars, and school programs.

DEVELOPMENT OFFICER   is in charge of raising money for the museum through the solicitation of individuals and corporations for donations of money; this person also plans, coordinates, and implements all fund-raising programs. Supervising the development staff is an additional responsibility.

MEMBERSHIP OFFICER   has the responsibility of attracting new members, retaining existing membership in the museum, and organizing special events and programs for the members. Duties can include the maintenance of membership records.

The American Association of Museums has also identified the following positions as museum-related jobs:

accountant	gardener/landscaper
archivist	graphic artist
artist	guard
attorney	historian
audiovisual technician	instructor
building superintendent	librarian
business manager	maintenance worker
clerk	model maker
computer specialist	personnel director
controller	public relations specialist
curatorial assistant	publications director
editor	research assistant
electrician	sales shop manager
filmmaker	secretary
food service manager	volunteer manager

Job Qualifications

For museum jobs, especially those actively involved in working in some way with the art collection, the key word in getting a job is *experience*. The two best ways to get needed experience are by participating in an internship program and serving as a volunteer. For art lovers aspiring to positions as directors, curators, educators, registrars, conservators, and librarians, master's degrees in museum studies, the museum's specialization, or in the applicants' work areas are generally expected. For some prestigious museums, only applicants with doctoral degrees are considered. Bachelor's degrees in business or arts administration are normally required for those seeking employment on the business side of art museums in such jobs as business manager, development officer, personnel director, and public relations specialist. Being affiliated with museum or professional associations is a plus for those seeking jobs in art museums. And since almost all jobs in museums require interaction with the public, from the guard talking to museum patrons to the director speaking to the board of the museum, good communication skills are necessary.

Salaries

Salaries of art museum workers are similar to those working in other museums. Employees at major museums will usually earn considerably more than those at small museums in towns or rural areas. Salaries will also depend on an individual's level of education and years of experience. Many individuals get their first positions in museums as unpaid interns or volunteers.

Here are the median salaries of employees in larger museums from a survey by the Association of Art Museum Directors.

Director	$103,000
Curator	$50,000
Senior Curator	$48,500
Curatorial Assistant	$22,600

A Look at Job Opportunities

Jobs in museums are attractive to art lovers, which results in keen competition for certain positions, as many applicants have the necessary training and subject knowledge and there are few openings. For example, candidates for curator positions may have to work part-time, as an intern or even as a volunteer assistant curator or research associate, after completing a formal education. In addition, jobs in museums are often subject to funding cuts during recessions or periods of budget tightening, reducing the demand for new employees. Overall, employment in museums is expected to increase as fast as the average for all occupations through the year 2006.

Director of a Smaller Art Museum

No one determines what the character of an art museum will be more than the director. In Saint Paul, Minnesota, Jim Czarniecki served as the director of the Minnesota Museum of American Art and determined that this museum would be people oriented. Under his leadership, the Museum School offered a formal instructional program in studio art and art history. And the scheduling of these classes was done to accommodate the variety of student needs and lifestyles: after-work classes for the downtown work crowd; traditional evening hours; and weekend workshops. The focus of the art in this museum is American art. Although the museum is people oriented, important research is not neglected. The staff is working on redefining American art and, through its research, is bringing out what has been ignored or repressed in the past.

Like most art museum directors, Jim had the responsibility for hiring and training support staff. Although the Minnesota Museum of Art can be considered a small or mid-sized museum, it had a staff of twenty-six full-time employees, fifteen part-time employees, and a faculty of twenty-five part-time teachers in the Museum School. One of Jim's duties as director was to interpret the board's policy for the staff and to design programs that would help the staff carry out this policy. Vision is required in the director's job: Jim was involved in setting goals and objectives for the museum to reach in the next three to five years. He was also the chief representative for the museum in the Twin Cities community, which required frequent dialog with community leaders in business and government.

Every day is different for the director of a museum. Jim spent 60 to 70 percent of his time working on all facets of the museum's campaign to raise $20 million to build a new facility. Much of his fund-raising time was spent talking to members of the board of trustees, donors, and key volunteers. One very appealing aspect of working in a museum this size is that directors are able to stay close to art. Jim was able to curate a show and be intimately involved in building the art collection.

Career Path

Although Jim was always interested in art and even took oil painting lessons in elementary school, he certainly did not expect to have a career in the arts. During high school, his interest was aeronautics, and he only took one art course. After graduation, Jim spent one year in Antwerp, Belgium, with the American Field Service program. During this year, his interest in art, especially photography, was reawakened. In college, Jim's major was physics, but he spent more time in the photography lab than the physics lab, as he was a photographer for both the newspaper and the yearbook. After graduation, jobs in physics were hard to find, and Jim finally determined that his interest was really photography and art. He elected to look for a job as a photographer.

Between interviews for photography jobs, Jim walked into the personnel office of the Art Institute of Chicago without an appointment and by the end of the day had a job with the Department of Education writing gallery guides and organizing a film and lecture series for a photography exhibition. Besides working at the Art Institute, Jim also enrolled part-time in classes to continue his education in art, especially in photography and filmmaking. Within two years, he was promoted to the position of supervisor of all public programs in the education department. His mentor at the museum allowed him to expand his knowledge of photography even further by letting him take time away from his job to do two internships in photography.

After three years of supervising programs at the Art Institute, the Ringling Museum of Art in Sarasota, Florida, offered Jim the job of director of education. He took the job because he saw it as an excellent opportunity to try out his ideas of making art more accessible to the public. He succeeded in bringing art to the people by establishing affiliate organizations with other museums in other cities and forming chapters of citizen volunteer groups that sponsored one or two exhibitions each year.

Jim's success with the Ringling program brought him an offer from patrons of the Mississippi Art Association to establish an art museum in Jackson and to serve as its director. They wanted someone who would create a museum that was very responsive to the public. Operating from an antebellum house with galleries in two parlors, Jim was able to help design the new museum and get it operating in eighteen months. Seven years later, the Minnesota Museum of Art asked Jim to serve as director.

Administrative Manager—Helping the Director

As administrative manager at the Minnesota Museum of American Art, Holly Metzler is assistant to the museum's director and works with all the departments. You might find her assisting the director of education in the library, helping the marketing department with a press release, or selecting books for the bookstore. She is also busy proofing newsletters to keep members and the board of directors updated on what is happening at the museum. In addition, Holly handles such administrative tasks as paying bills and handling employee benefits.

Holly is a recent college graduate who was able to secure this great position for art lovers because she possessed impressive qualifications. She had a bachelor's degree in English, showing that she could handle the writing side of this job, plus she had taken many classes in art history in college. Holly also had gained experience in museum work by volunteering as a gallery assistant and a curatorial assistant. Her business background was equally solid because she'd run her own business while in school.

Career Path

Holly points out that getting a position as an administrative assistant at a small museum gives you a great opportunity to learn how each department of a museum functions. However, to climb the ladder, even in a small museum, she says that it is advisable to have more education than a bachelor's degree. She is currently attending a workshop in modern art and plans to take more technical writing and computer skills courses. Holly also hopes to return to school in the future and obtain a master's degree in art history, theory, and criticism.

Curators—Guardians of Art

Beyond researching and interpreting the art in their care and arranging exhibitions, curators are the keepers of the art heritage that resides in museums. The number of curators in an art museum is closely tied to the size of the museum. In a large museum like the Fine Arts Museums of San Francisco, the curatorial career path is outlined in the diagram.

A similar career path will be found in mid-sized museums; however, in very small museums there may not be any specifically named curatorial positions, as the director may also serve as the curator.

Curator of the Textile Department

Melissa Leventon is the curator of the textile department of the Fine Arts Museums of San Francisco. In this position, she has the mandate of caring for fifteen thousand textiles and costumes from all over the world. To help in this task, she has an associate curator. Although her department does not have a formal intern program, unpaid interns frequently work in the department when a suitable project arises. Melissa advises art lovers who are interested in her field to get a taste of what it is like by serving as interns or volunteers.

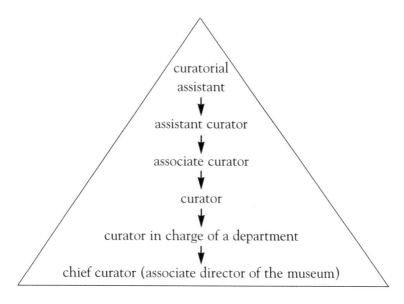

A curator's job is a multifaceted one in which the day's tasks vary. Melissa is involved in researching, writing, and cataloging, which means spending considerable time on the computer. Melissa also has the responsibility of looking for new pieces to add to the collection and raising funds. Like most curators, she has the challenge of coming up with ideas for exhibitions. This is a big task in her department as there are usually two new exhibits in the costume gallery, two in the ethnographic textiles gallery, and one in the tapestries gallery every year. Plus, every two or three years, Melissa sets up a big exhibition. The current one relates to food while the previous one was an outstanding exhibition—The Mystery of the Dead Sea Scrolls—that was widely acclaimed. Arranging for a new exhibit can take from six to thirty-six months, while installing the exhibit may require from one day to three weeks. It is important for prospective curators to understand that besides being involved with art in some way, this job also requires considerable administrative work.

Career Path

Melissa has always been fascinated by what people wear; she made a lot of costumes for theatrical productions in high school. When she entered the job market, she was well prepared with a bachelor's degree in English and a master's in the history of dress. Her first position was as a curatorial assistant in costumes and textiles at the Museum of London. Then she became an assistant curator for the department where she is now curator.

Conservators—Advocates for All Works of Art

Conservators are the experts who are interested primarily in the welfare of works of art. Their job is to prevent deterioration and repair paintings, sculptures, books, textiles, rugs, tapestries, picture frames, porcelains, other fine works of art, and cultural properties. Conservators usually have a specialty, since the problems to be resolved in caring for works of art are so difficult that no individual can be an expert in restoring all kinds of art. Preserving a two thousand-year-old carving found in the ocean and preserving a fifteenth-century porcelain vase are two very different tasks.

Educational Requirements

Becoming a conservator is a lengthy process, whether art lovers do it through a formal school program or through an apprenticeship that will last a minimum of five years and usually extend to eight years. There are no undergraduate programs that give bachelor's degrees in conservation. However, it is possible to take technical studies at the undergraduate level and then enter an apprentice or master's program. The first step in the academic approach is to get a bachelor's degree, usually in art history, which should be coupled with undergraduate courses in chemistry, physics, geology, biology, and studio art. Obtaining a master's degree in a conservator's program in some areas of study is quite difficult because of the limited number of schools and limited number of applicants accepted into programs. For example, there are just three schools in the United States that offer a master's degree in fine arts conservation, and each accepts only a very small number of students. Therefore, most students have to wait two to three years to enter a master's program in this area. During that time, they are expected to gain experience working for a conservator. After graduation, they will need to serve in an internship. Check your library for a listing of schools offering conservation programs, and you can write to the American Institute for Conservation, 1400 Sixteenth Street NW, Suite 340, Washington, DC 20036, requesting career information.

A Conservator of Fine Art

Larger museums have laboratories where conservators work. Smaller museums either tap into the resources of the larger museums or use private conservators. Scott M. Haskins is a conservator who directs a fine art conservation laboratory. His area of expertise in conservation is fine paintings and works of art on paper. Scott's clients include museums of all types; city, state, and federal goverments; historical societies; corporations with large art holdings; and holders of private collections. Scott trained in Italy and obtained the equivalent of a master's degree in fine arts conservation, followed by a one-year internship.

In his conservation work, Scott is involved in such tasks as taking water stains out of a seventeenth century drawing, cleaning and repairing rips in paintings, taking acid stains out of watercolors, repairing and preserving frames, and stopping the deterioration of paintings and works of art on paper. He is interested in every aspect of an art work's welfare. He sees that it is shipped and stored correctly and advises clients on how to prevent light and pollution damage to paintings. Art scholars also use him as a consultant in determining the authenticity of works of art. He was able to tell one scholar that a work of art supposedly by Goya could not be genuine because the whites used in the painting were not invented until 1927.

Scott also has administrative responsibilities. He supervises a conservator and an apprentice with a master's degree in art history and sets up the daily work schedule for the laboratory. A very important part of his job is making sure that all work done on art in the laboratory is carefully documented. In addition, he will spend time talking to clients and prospective clients.

Scott has truly found a perfect career for art lovers as he is preserving what they cherish. The outlook for jobs is good for conservators. Museums seek these highly trained professionals for staff positions or as consultants. Because so much still has to be learned about how to conserve works of art, employment opportunities are also good for conservation scientists who research the effects of such things as pollution, humidity, and lighting on works of art.

Exhibit Designers—Experts in Displaying Art

Exhibit designers do more than prepare works of art for display in a museum; they also prepare the space to hold the works of art. The designers are responsible for the lighting, color of the walls, support graphics for the works of art, audiovisual materials, flow of traffic, and security for an exhibit. They must also see that the exhibit tells a story with a beginning, middle, and end.

Sherman O'Hara is the chief exhibits designer at the Indianapolis Museum of Art, in charge of the more than thirty new
exhibits featured in the museum each year. He works directly on
the installation of eight exhibits a year. His work year is rather
like show business, "another opening, another show." Each
installation begins with a curator telling him or one of the
designers on his staff what the story line of the exhibit will be. In
many museums, the curator, exhibits designer, and educator will
plan the exhibit story together. The next step is for the exhibits
designer to plan the actual exhibit, which must be approved by
the curator. Then a drawing of the exhibit is made. The final step
is the installation of the exhibit. This is done by a team including the designer, a lighting technician, someone who mounts the
paintings, and other necessary technicians. At times, the museum exhibits "packaged" shows that already come with a story
line. In this case, the designer will tailor the exhibit to fit the
space.

Sherman has a staff of seven in his department. Two of these
people are exhibits designers. When the schedule of exhibits is
published for the year, the designers will choose or be assigned to
the exhibits they will do during the year. In the past ten years,
the career of exhibits designer has become more professional.
There is now a standing committee of exhibits designers on the
board of the American Association of Museums. And designers
now have a professional organization—the National Association
of Museum Exhibitors. There is no specific course work that is
recognized as preparation for this career. Most designers have a
bachelor's or master's degree in fine arts with an architectural or
design background. As this profession has become more disci-
plined, there are now opportunities for internships in this area in
museums. Sherman now has one intern each year. Being an
intern is an excellent way to get experience in this area.

Being the chief exhibits designer means that Sherman has
considerable paperwork. He manages his department's budget,
handles correspondence, and orders materials. He also has to

plan and attend meetings and make sure that exhibits are installed on schedule.

Career Path

Sherman originally considered a career in accounting and actually graduated as a business major. After graduation, he changed his mind and went to a school of design for postgraduate work. Then he and a partner started a space design business. After they sold the business, he traveled and then took a job at the Indianapolis Museum of Art as chief exhibits designer—the same job he holds today.

Educator—A Performance Arts Coordinator

Anna Thompson learned about a position at the Indianapolis Museum of Art through a newspaper advertisement. The ad read: "The Indianapolis Museum of Art has an opening for a full-time music performance arts coordinator. We are seeking an experienced educator with a background in music and/or music and film to research, develop, and implement the music, film, and performance arts programs for the museum. Many programs are designed in conjunction with educational programming for the permanent collection and special exhibitions. Concerts and film series are presented on weekends and evenings. Master's degree in music or related fields is highly desirable. Three to five years university or high school teaching experience or equivalent. Background in film study or art history also desirable. Strong oral, written, communication, and organizational skills required."

Anna had been a school music teacher for three years, held an advanced degree in library science, and had experience in organizing educational programs at the library and making arrangements for a meeting of the National Conference of Music

Librarians, which qualified her for the position. She applied and was hired. Her job involved dealing with several media—art, music, and film. Anna researched and developed programs related to specific art exhibits. She selected films for the summer film series. In addition, she put together family programs and programs that were sent out to the schools. When the museum's new pavilion opened, Anna commissioned a work by a composer to reflect the artist's work in the exhibition. In this job, she also did grant proposal writing to obtain funds for the performing arts programs. In carrying out her job, she worked closely with the museum's curators.

Deputy Director for Development

The Fine Arts Museums of San Francisco include the de Young Museum for American Art and the California Palace of the Legion of Honor, which has a European collection. Housed in two buildings, it is one of the largest museums in the United States, with a budget of $13.5 million a year. The development office has a director, an associate director, and two deputy directors who are in charge of all unearned revenue—grants and contributions from individuals, corporations, foundations, and government agencies. The directors have the responsibility of running a program that instills good relations between the museum's benefactors and the museum.

Jim Forbes is a deputy director at the Fine Arts Museums of San Francisco. While he was working on his doctorate in music history, Jim decided he did not want to stay in the academic world as a teacher but preferred to work in arts administration. For him, the idea of working in a development office was especially appealing, as he realized the importance of funding to the continued operation of programs in all the arts. He became more aware of the important work done by development officers by volunteering in the development office of the university while he was a graduate student.

Jim first secured a job as chief development officer with a small ballet company. A friend in the development office of the university told him about this job opening. Jim made his next career move to the development office of the Nelson Atkins Museum in Kansas City because he was interested in working in the visual arts. A search team called him about the job opening for his current position as deputy director of the Fine Arts Museums of San Francisco.

The directors of the development office do not do any direct fund-raising at the Fine Arts Museums of San Francisco. Instead, Jim works with board members and board committees who actually do the fund-raising. Jim and his staff of four do all the support work for the fund-raisers. They educate the board about the museum's needs, prepare brochures to tell the museum's story, create mail solicitations, plan special exhibitions, and devise the year's fund-raising strategy. And when corporations give gifts, Jim's staff finalizes the agreements. Art lovers who want to find a career that really supports the operation of museums will find careers in development offices to be very rewarding.

Human Resources Manager at the Walker Art Center

Almost every member of the administrative staff at the Walker Art Center in Minneapolis, Minnesota, is an artist who brings an artist's sensitivity to his or her position. Wendy Lane, the human resources manager at the museum, is no exception. Art is so important to her that she lives in a studio with both living and work space. She meets once a month with other artists to critique each other's work.

In her job as human resources manager, her primary responsibility is recruitment. When a new staff member is needed, she writes the job description and then sees that the opening is publicized. This involves sending the posting to about 350 arts and service organizations as well as placing ads. Wendy handles the response by reviewing resumes and working with the supervisor of the open position to decide who will be interviewed. The supervisor does the initial interview, and Wendy does the final interview before they get together to make a decision. The demand for positions at the very prestigious Walker Art Center is huge. Hundreds will apply for every position, especially since many artists want to work at art museums. Just having a background in art is not a sufficient qualification for most positions. Applicants generally need to have bachelor's degrees, with advanced degrees preferable for many positions.

Besides her recruitment responsibilities, Wendy is in charge of new employee orientation. She talks to new employees about the museum's policies and procedures and signs them up for benefits. And when an employee leaves, she will do the exit interview and the paperwork on the termination. As part of her job, she has written the policy and procedures booklet and created an employee appraisal form that is tied to annual salary increases. She also makes up salary guidelines that are approved by supervisors. Wendy wrote the museum's affirmative action plan and makes sure that it is being followed. It is also her job to respond to discrimination issues. Wendy's responsibilities include serving as liaison between employees and management and managing the personnel procurement budget and the personal services budget for things that benefit employees in general.

Career Path

With a bachelor's degree in arts administration, Wendy had the academic background necessary for obtaining an administrative job at a museum. But she also had an additional strength— business experience from being the co-owner of a health food distribution company. Wendy answered a newspaper ad for a secretary at the Walker. Her prospective boss also wanted someone who could handle the human resources part of his job and thought she would be able to do this. Within one year, she was an administrative assistant, and three years later she was the human resources manager. Wendy's career path shows how a fulfilling career in an art museum can develop from an entry-level position.

Job Opportunities in Human Resources

The opportunity to obtain a job as human resources manager in an art museum is limited because only museums with one hundred or more employees will need a full-time staff member in this position. Quite often, this position is coupled with that of administrative director. While a salary of $25,000 to $30,000 would be paid for human resources managers at art museums, the same position in for-profit organizations would command a salary of between $40,000 and $60,000.

Art Galleries—Working Amidst Art

Art lovers can purchase sculpture, etchings, antique prints, original fine art, tribal art, serigraphs, and limited edition graphics at art galleries. They can also find jobs working in art galleries, for there are thousands of them in the United States. Furthermore, there is such a diversity in galleries that art lovers can look for a job in a gallery that sells the art of their favorite media, styles, periods, or artists.

Art galleries can be as dissimilar as, on the one hand, a small showroom in a tourist resort selling paintings and sculpture by local artists versus a ten thousand-square-foot loft in a high-rent district in New York City selling paintings worth millions of dollars, on the other. Wherever art lovers choose to work, it is essential that they have a knowledge of art. At many galleries, this means having at least a bachelor's degree in art history, and for some galleries having a master's degree is required even for entry-level positions. In New York City, competition is so intense that job seekers try to get a foot in the door by working as interns for no wages or minimum wage or by taking the most lowly job available at a gallery.

Gallery Director in a Midwestern City

Several years ago, Eckert Fine Art had both antique furniture and nineteenth and twentieth century paintings with a few eighteenth century pieces. As the owners of the gallery acquired exceptional estates that had paintings by renowned artists of the region, the gallery emerged as an art gallery that solely promoted the painting of regional artists, past and present. Today, the gallery has tripled in size and now also deals in nationally known American and European artists who paint in the traditional style.

From childhood, Jim Ross, the director of the gallery, has had a keen interest in art and has always painted and sketched. Fortunately for this true aficionado of art, his jobs have always been associated with art in some way. While in college at the Herron School of Art, he worked at the Indianapolis Museum of Art in advertising and marketing. Then after graduating with a degree in visual communication, he continued to work at the museum until he left to form his own graphic design firm. Jim became acquainted with the gallery owners where he now works through doing brochures for them. When the firm moved to more spacious quarters, he even helped the owners move. Shortly thereafter, he became assistant to the director of the gallery and then assumed his present position when the director left.

On the Job

As director of the gallery, Jim is able to spend his days working with art. He does not have to deal with administrative tasks, as they are handled by an office manager. Jim spends most of his time selling art. This includes talking to clients in the gallery and on the phone. He acts as their consultant and guide in the purchase of paintings and will even go to their homes to hang paintings. Another aspect of his job is acquiring art for the gallery. Because there is a limited supply of art the gallery sells, part of his job is convincing people to sell their art. As the gallery has acquired a solid reputation for selling fine art, this task has become easier as more people wish to sell their art to the gallery.

Career Advice

Young art lovers should try to become acquainted with individuals who work with art. Knowing the owners of the gallery gave Jim the opportunity to demonstrate his expertise with art and find his current job.

Gallery Owner in New York City

Major art galleries in New York City are extremely selective in choosing entry-level employees. Armed with a bachelor's degree in art history plus experience as a summer intern at the Metropolitan Museum of Art, Tim Nye went around to art galleries with his impressive resume looking for his first job. He found a job as a gallery assistant at Nancy Hoffman Gallery, where he handled art, made boxes for shipping, sent out packages, labeled slides, and went to clients' homes to hang art they had purchased. There was no glamour in this job, but it was a beginning for Tim. His next job was as a cataloger at Robert Miller Gallery. A cataloging job involves taking photographs of art and writing the serial numbers on the back of the work. This was a particularly appropriate job since Tim had written his thesis on one of the artists whose work was sold at this gallery.

Tim went away from the art world briefly to get an M.B.A. with a concentration in nonprofit organizations. He knew that he always wanted to return to the art world and did so during the summer after his first year of graduate school. With profits made from selling two paintings by a pop artist whose work swiftly escalated in price after the death of Andy Warhol, Tim was able to mount his own exhibition. He rented a temporary gallery space and put together a showing called "Three Painters." One of the painters was a friend, Paul Pagk, who had received recognition in France. After graduation from business school, Tim found a fabulous seventy-five hundred-square-foot open loft. He was also able to obtain funding from a foundation for two one-person shows in his loft gallery. Each show was hung for about six weeks, longer than the typical one-month show in New York City. The success of previous shows allowed him to find funding for a third show, the works of a sculptor. Tim is trying to make his gallery a center for contemporary arts and is holding poetry readings and concerts in the gallery. As far as the future goes, Tim hopes that he will be selling art and continuing with his gallery.

More Careers for Art Lovers

Artists' Representatives

Both commercial and fine artists often need someone to bring them jobs. This is the role artists' representatives play: they sell artists' talents to people in a position to pay for the use of their talents. Shirley Talbert works full-time as a representative for commercial artists. Although she works in a firm that has another representative, most representatives work alone. To find companies that need commercial artists, she calls on art directors in advertising agencies, graphic designers, and corporations, talking to them about their needs. Her clientele is decidedly not a fixed group, and neither is the group of artists she represents, with new people always needing her services. Commercial artists call Shirley or send her resumes of their work. She evaluates their artwork and tries to sign contracts for at least a year with the artists she decides to represent.

Much time and effort is required to market the work of an artist. Shirley works with the artist to create a portfolio that displays his or her distinctive style, which she can then show potential users of the artist's work. When a client requests an artist who can do a certain type of work, Shirley usually visits the client with the portfolios of three artists who have different styles. Her job as an artist representative does not end when an artist is selected by a client. She is responsible for seeing that the artist's work is completed on time and to the specifications of her client.

Shirley also works part-time on her own as a fine-artist representative. In this role, she finds a client first and then looks for an artist after spending considerable time consulting with the client on his or her needs. Being an artist's representative requires both business and art backgrounds, which Shirley has. Her business experience is derived from working in marketing after she graduated from college with a bachelor's degree in sales and marketing. Shirley acquired her knowledge of art through collecting paintings and graphics.

Art Advisors

Many people love art and would like to have excellent pieces of art in their homes. Communities often want to put on art exhibits for their residents. Corporations frequently want to have art collections. Governmental units often want paintings, sculptures, mosaics, and murals to decorate buildings. Because everyone is not an expert at selecting art, the career of art advisor has emerged. Art advisors are the experts who help people and organizations find the art they want. They do not deal in art or have an inventory of art. Their job is to be advisors. They can work alone or with a group.

Lynne Bear is an art advisor who works alone out of a home office. Most of her business is focused on helping organizations find art to be displayed in public places. She also advises individuals in the selection of art. In order to do this, she has a wide network of contacts in the art community that enables her to find the artwork that her clients want. She both buys art for clients and commissions artists to create pieces. In addition, she puts together works of art for exhibitions.

Career Path

Unlike many art lovers, Lynne was not always interested in art. It came to her later as an adult when she visited museums for the very first time during a trip to Europe. On her return to the United States, Lynne set out to learn more about art, first by volunteering at museums and then by obtaining a master's degree in art history. Her first job in the art world was at a large regional auction house where she started as the assistant director of painting with the responsibility of appraising art, finding works of art, and selling art. Before she left the firm to start her own business, she had become director of the fine arts department and had made excellent contacts within the art community.

Career Advice

Lynne advises people who want to have a job like hers to study the field of art history in an academic environment to gain a historic and aesthetic perspective as well as to get experience in a structured environment to gain the skills they will need. She believes that working in an auction house is an excellent way to learn a lot about art.

Art Appraisers

People often want to know the value of a work of art for buying or selling the piece or sometimes just to satisfy their curiosity. In addition, they may want information for insurance, tax, or family division purposes. The experts who decide the price or value of artwork are called appraisers. This career requires really knowing art and the value of individual pieces of art.

Karen Tallackson was about eighteen when she decided that she wanted to be an art appraiser. To acquire the necessary background in art, she obtained both bachelor's and master's degrees in art history. She also studied art in England and France, where she had direct contact with many works of fine art. To begin to have an idea of the value of different pieces, she read such periodicals as *Connoisseur*, *Art News*, *Art in America*, and *Art and Antiques*. To gain more knowledge of art and valuing art, she started at Butterfield & Butterfield, a firm of international fine art auctioneers and appraisers, as an intern and became an appraiser with this company. Her internship project was to create a chronological dictionary of California paintings. This helped Karen become familiar with the artists and their styles, as well as previous auction prices of their works. When her internship was completed, Karen became administrative assistant to the director. This allowed her to become familiar with the clientele of the auction house and auction procedures.

After Karen expressed an interest in contemporary art, the firm let her start making appraisals from photographs of contemporary art that were sent to the firm for evaluation. In her next position as inventory manager, she inventoried every piece of art that came into the firm by entering it into the computer. This meant she was actually seeing and handling works of art. According to Karen, the more art a prospective appraiser sees, the more skilled the individual becomes in making qualitative judgments. She also learned more about the market by talking to clients. One way prospective appraisers can find out more about the job is by contacting the American Society of Appraisers, which has an organization that students can join. This organization also gives accreditation to professional appraisers. For more information about appraising contact the American Society of Appraisers, P.O. Box 17264, Washington, DC 20041.

On the Way to Becoming an Appraiser

After the contemporary art appraiser left the firm, Karen became Butterfield & Butterfield's contemporary art appraiser. One of her duties was to make insurance appraisals. She also found properties for the firm's semiannual contemporary art auctions. She acquired properties for these sales from all over the country, which meant spending considerable time on the phone. When a piece arrived at the firm, Karen had it photographed and entered information about it on the computer. For each auction, she created the catalog that described the artist, the work of art, and the pre-auction estimate. Appraisers must know the market, so Karen was always going to galleries and openings plus reading *Journal of Art* and *International Art Newsletter* to keep abreast of pricing and market trends. Karen left her job at Butterfield & Butterfield to work for a company trying to put art on-line.

Being an appraiser is an opportunity for art lovers to have daily contact with art. Besides requiring an excellent knowledge of the media that the appraiser values, phone and computer skills are essential, as is an ability to deal with people.

Fine Art Auctioneers

An auction at Butterfield & Butterfield is a sale at which people bid for fine art, antiques, jewelry, and collectibles. One of the auctioneers is Bernard Osher, who is also owner and chairman of this firm. To prepare for an auction, he must be aware of what is being sold. This means studying the catalog for the auction and learning which items are most important. It also involves talking with department people about the items to be auctioned.

You do not go to school to become an auctioneer. Instead, you learn by watching other auctioneers and then developing your own style. A very important characteristic for auctioneers is self-confidence. Before Bernard Osher became an auctioneer, he was an art collector. He had attended many auctions and became an auctioneer as soon as he and his partner purchased the firm.

Art Critics

According to David Bonetti, art critic for the *San Francisco Examiner*, art critics can be divided into two groups. In one group, you will find the critics who write for art journals. Their audience is assumed to be knowledgeable about art, so jargon can be used in these critics' pieces. The other group of art critics write for daily or weekly newspapers with large circulations. They cannot assume that their readers have any more than a basic knowledge of art, so they write in a straightforward way, reporting on what is happening in art. Some newspaper art critics just report the facts. Others, like David, write more about what artists are trying to do and whether they are successful in achieving their own goals. He also feels it is important to explain to his readers what the newest art is all about.

Unlike music and theater critics on newspaper staffs, art critics seldom have an overnight deadline. It is not as important for them to report immediately on the opening of a new show at a gallery or museum because people will have many opportunities to see the show. Not having the pressure of a deadline gives the art critic time to reflect on a new show.

As sole art critic for the *Examiner*, David writes three or four columns a week. His job should be very appealing to art lovers because he spends considerable time looking at art in museums, galleries, and other places that exhibit. Much reading about art is required in his work. For example, an exhibit of Indonesian art at a museum had a four hundred-page catalog that David had to study to learn about the background, history, aesthetics, and cultural context of the exhibit. In the case of contemporary art there is rarely a catalog, so he had to research his response to the art—which may itself become part of a future catalog.

Unfortunately, there are not a great number of jobs for art critics at newspapers, since only major newspapers will have full-time critics. In addition, the outlook for more newspaper jobs for art critics is not rosy. The number of newspapers in the United States is steadily dropping, with approximately one thousand fewer newspapers today than in the early 1900s. Furthermore, many major newspapers are losing circulation to suburban papers.

Career Path

There is no one career route to becoming an art critic at a newspaper. It is not something that can be studied at school. Obviously, an ability to write and a knowledge of art are basic requirements. Many art critics, according to David, started out wanting to be artists or writers—especially poets—and then redirected their interests to critical writing. However, David's route to becoming an art critic did not develop in this way. After majoring in literature and taking many art courses in college, he taught preschool—specializing in art and literature. From teaching he went to work in sales at an art gallery. While working in the gallery, he started writing art reviews for a monthly publication. He heard of an opening at a Boston paper for an art critic, sent them his clippings, and got the job. His next career move was to his current position in San Francisco. "Being an art critic," David says, "is being paid to work with my interest." It is decidedly not a nine-to-five job for him. Even on off days he is at galleries and museums pursuing his interest in art.

Art Teachers

While a very limited number of art students ultimately become professional artists, most gain an appreciation of art through their classes in school. Art lovers who wish to share their love of art with others will find teaching art a rewarding career. Teaching lets practicing art lovers introduce future art lovers to different media and the history of art and artists through the ages.

Qualifications

Individuals wishing to teach art in public schools will need bachelor's degrees in education with training in art education. Most will also obtain their master's degrees early in their teaching careers. At the college or university level, having a doctorate is a prerequisite for all art teachers except those who have attained acclaim as outstanding artists.

Demand

Art lovers wishing to teach in elementary school will find that the current demand for art teachers is reduced in many areas because of budget cutting. At the high school level, fewer art teachers are needed in many states because more required courses have been added to the curriculum, which means fewer students can choose art classes as electives. Competition for positions teaching art in colleges and universities is as intense as it is in all other areas of instruction at this level.

Salaries

While the average salary for all teachers is currently approaching $40,000 a year, it is important to remember that beginning teachers often have salaries in the low- to mid-$20,000 range. Then with each year of experience, their salaries climb according to the salary scale of the school district. Salaries also increase as teachers gain additional degrees or college units. Private school teachers generally earn less than public school teachers.

Art from the Cart

Sonia Fernandez is an elementary school art teacher. She has taught in beautiful, fully equipped art rooms, in cafeterias, and in science rooms; she has also pushed a cart loaded with art supplies from room to room. Teaching art can be a hectic experience in an elementary school. Art teachers never seem to have enough time to get everything done. Supplies have to be taken out and put back for each class, and a project must be completed in thirty or forty-five minutes. According to Sonia, an hour would be an ideal amount of time for an art class, especially for students in the intermediate grades, but this rarely happens. Art lovers planning to teach art should also realize that they may see every student in the school during the course of the week. This often means teaching art to more than five hundred students. Art teachers also have demands made on their time to prepare such things as posters for paper drives and props or scenery for a school musical or play, plus helping children participate in art competitions. Add in the frustration of crowded classrooms, and you might wonder why Sonia enjoys teaching art and would not think of teaching any other class. The reason is simple: she thoroughly enjoys introducing young children to the world of art.

A Lifetime of Teaching Art

Jim Doversberger always knew he wanted to be an art teacher, and that is the one and only job he has ever had except for a short stint in the navy. Jim brought a solid knowledge of art to his teaching career, since he earned both bachelor's and master's degrees in fine arts. He took education courses and did student teaching to qualify for his teaching credential. While attending Herron Art School, he taught art classes every Saturday morning. He continued teaching these classes for many years after he became a full-time teacher because he liked teaching classes to children of different ages.

Jim first learned of his future teaching job from a notice on the bulletin board at the art school. Prospective art teachers can still learn about positions in this way, as well as through college placement offices and even newspaper ads. Jim applied for the job and was hired as an art teacher. When he first started at Lawrence Central High School, he was the only art teacher at this small suburban high school. Over the course of his career, the suburb grew and the art faculty expanded until there were six art teachers and Jim was department chair. The number of art teachers was reduced when another high school was built in the district and further reduced to one full-time position and one part-time position when fewer students began to take art because of increased requirements in science and social studies.

A typical course load for Jim would be teaching beginning art, drawing, and graphics; intermediate drawing and painting; and advanced art. His classes would average twenty-six students at the beginning level, but as few as twelve on the advanced level. On the intermediate level, Jim would always devote Friday to teaching art history. He and the other art teachers in the district had the opportunity to develop their own curriculums within the broad guidelines of the state requirements. Most experienced teachers will be able to develop their own curriculums in this way.

Art teachers, like other teachers, have responsibilities that extend beyond the classroom. Jim sponsored an art club at times throughout his career; in the early part of his career, before a stagecraft teacher was hired, he designed the stage sets for the school's two annual productions. When an empty room turned up at the school, he established an art gallery that featured constant shows of the students' artwork. Much time every year was devoted to helping students prepare for major art competitions. He was also on the board of the regional scholastic art competition. Some of his time was also spent judging other competitions.

Jim spent considerable time painting at the start of his teaching career. Then this lover of the arts switched his interest to the local theater and appeared in more than sixty-five plays. Teaching does give art lovers time to pursue their interests in the summer. Jim frequently traveled to Europe to visit art museums. He also attended workshops during the summer.

Additional Career Options

Wherever a collection of art is located, there exist possible jobs for art lovers. Art lovers should investigate the possibilities of working at corporations because these places, like museums and art galleries, may have art collections that require curators, conservators, art historians, and librarians. For example, Bank of America and Goldman Sachs & Company have sizeable art collections that are predominantly displayed in the firms' hallways and offices. Curators of collections in the corporate world, besides loaning pieces to employees for their offices, often launch programs to educate employees about art.

Today's libraries also offer job opportunities for art lovers. Many libraries have programs that involve the loaning of works of art. In addition, librarians with a knowledge of art are needed in the art departments of major libraries.

Beyond the world of fine art, there is the rather large world of commercial art. You can imagine the size of this world when you think of all the commercials that bombard you from billboards, newspapers, magazines, catalogs, and radio and television stations. In each of these arenas, there are scores of employees dealing with the development of commercial art designed to sell products to the public. Many jobs, especially in advertising agencies and commercial art studios, involve working directly with art.

Whenever art lovers see art that appeals to them, they are also seeing job opportunities in buying, selling, displaying, and choosing this art. Being involved in art is not just a job for its creators.

CHAPTER THREE

Careers for Music Lovers

Enjoying the Beat

"If music be the food of love, play on;
Give me excess of it..." SHAKESPEARE, *Twelfth Night*

M usic has played a key role in cultures from those of ancient civilizations to our twenty-first-century world. Six thousand years ago in Egypt, court musicians were playing harps and wind and percussion instruments while military bands used trumpets and drums. In our modern world, music continues to play an important role in ceremonial occasions from White House receptions to parades. It also occupies a significant place in such disparate activities as preschoolers singing "Twinkle, Twinkle, Little Star" to teenagers dancing to rock 'n' roll to adults enjoying symphonies and operas.

In recent years, music has turned into a multibillion dollar business offering careers to thousands of people. There are opportunities to work with a symphony, opera, or ballet company; in radio and television; in the recording and record business; with music retailers and wholesalers; in education; and in the creation, repair, and restoration of musical instruments. Wherever music is played, created, sold, or enjoyed, music lovers should investigate career opportunities. You do not need to be a trained musician to have a job in the music world. Many jobs exist on the business side for staff publicists, promotion managers, music shop salespersons, personal managers, booking agents, and business managers. Just a glance at the music section in the yellow pages of your local telephone directory will give you an idea of the number of companies in your community that are connected with music.

While music is a performing art, few individuals are able to support themselves as full-time performers. Many musicians elect to combine performing with jobs that allow them to be closely associated with music in the workplace. They can be employed as music teachers, music therapists, copyists, recording engineers, instrument restorers, disc jockeys, librarians, choir directors, arrangers, and in an amazing variety of other jobs closely associated with music.

Teaching Music

Teaching music is an excellent way to share a love of music with others—from fledgling musicians in preschool to skilled graduate students in a university. Since each age level offers different challenges and rewards, prospective music teachers will need to decide which age group is most appealing to them. At all levels, music teachers in schools have a number of duties that must be performed, from taking attendance to giving grades. In addition, there are frequently state, local, or school guidelines that prescribe the curriculum that is to be taught in music classes. Besides normal teaching duties, most music teachers will usually spend time before and after school working with different musical groups or preparing students for special contests and performances.

You can learn more about careers in teaching music by contacting the following organization and requesting information on careers in music: Music Educators National Conference (MENC), 1806 Robert Fulton Drive, Reston, VA 20191-4348. Or visit the Web site at http://www.menc.org, which has information about jobs and preparing for jobs in music education.

You can also learn more about the profession by studying professional journals like these publications found in university libraries and some public libraries:

The American Music Teacher

The American String Teacher

Music Educators' Journal

The Choral Journal

Contributions to Music Education

Besides information on teaching, a few of these journals have some job listings for music teachers. Libraries also have state publications concerned with music education that will frequently have advertisements for teaching positions.

Job Qualifications and Opportunities

Elementary and secondary school music teachers normally hold bachelor's degrees with majors in music education. During the course of their teaching careers, many will also obtain master's degrees. Current funding difficulties in the public schools, coupled with the fact that music is not considered a basic subject, have led to a tighter job market for prospective music teachers. Individuals seeking employment as music teachers usually learn of job opportunities through college placement bureaus, employment fairs, newspaper advertisements, and networking with other teachers. Many also contact school districts to see if there are positions available for music teachers.

College and university music teachers who teach theory classes are usually required to have a doctorate in some aspect of music; however, exceptions are made for those who teach performance classes if they have the press clippings to demonstrate a national reputation in their teaching areas. Competition is extremely intense for positions at this level, and many qualified people are competing for few jobs.

Salaries

The average salary of music teachers in public schools is the same as that of all other teachers. Experienced teachers can earn close to $40,000, while beginning teachers may start with salaries in the low-$20,000 range.

Teaching in an Elementary School

Julia Scherer has taught music at the same elementary school for more than twenty years. She plans to stay at this school until she takes early retirement to publish the school musicals she has written and to make commercials. Not able to find a job as a music teacher after graduation from college with a bachelor's degree in music education, Julia applied for a job as a substitute teacher— only to find the district was looking for a music teacher. She applied for the job, was hired, and is still working at this school. Like most music teachers, Julia has obtained a master's degree in music and has taken other additional courses.

As an elementary music specialist, Julia teaches general music classes that feature instruction in vocal music, composers, music reading, instruments of the orchestra, music appreciation, and playing the recorder—depending on the grade levels of her students. Outside of her hours at school, she spends time planning and presenting three major musicals, two spring sings, and choir and recorder ensemble programs each year. Twice a week, she comes in early to give special instruction to the ensemble groups. Most elementary school music teachers will have similar responsibilities.

Inspired by her elementary and high school music teachers to choose a career as a music teacher, Julia transmits her love of music to her students. She was introduced by one of her former students, who had a major role in the musical *Cats,* to the cast backstage as the lady who got him started in music. Knowing her students appreciate her efforts is what makes her career so satisfying.

Julia resembles most music teachers in that her involvement with music does not end in the classroom. Over the years, she has directed children's church choirs, given private voice lessons, sung with an entertainment company, and starred in numerous community theater productions, receiving many awards for her singing and acting ability in these shows.

Teaching in a Junior High School

It is a challenging job to create an orchestra, choir, or band from a group of students in sixth, seventh, and eighth grades. Many of these students have never sung a note or held a musical instrument in their hands before the first day in the music classroom. This is a challenge that faces junior high school music teachers like Joe Zaharako every day.

Joe is the band director at a large junior high school. His teaching responsibilities include teaching band to students in sixth, seventh, and eighth grades, along with a general music class for sixth graders. Other teachers at this school concentrate on teaching choir or orchestra, along with a few classes in general music. At smaller schools, music teachers should expect to teach both vocal and instrumental music classes.

One of the most appealing aspects of Joe's job is seeing how his students develop as musicians during the three years they spend at the school where he teaches. Most school districts will not have the sixth grade as part of the junior high school, and increasingly there are middle schools with just seventh and eighth grades.

Joe's educational background includes a bachelor's degree and a master's degree in music education, the typical education pattern for music teachers. His time spent with music is not limited to teaching; he is also a member of a brass choir.

Teaching in a High School

Thomas Dick was not born into a musically inclined family; his father did not even recognize a cello when his son brought one home. However, from an early age music just seemed like the natural thing for Thomas to do. He became a very skilled cellist, playing first chair in several community orchestras. During college, he made the decision to become a teacher rather than a performer because he wanted to help young people. He was able to pay for his education with a music scholarship plus jobs as a cellist with a symphony orchestra and as a string bass player in a group that performed at supper clubs. Thomas also played in the orchestra for road shows like *Fiddler on the Roof* and *Sound of Music*. You will find that a great number of music teachers earned part of their college costs through working as performers.

Since completing his bachelor's degree in music education, Thomas has taught at three high schools, obtaining his master's degree in music education along the way. In his present job, he is the director of orchestras at a large suburban high school. He teaches four periods of strings and one period of wind and percussion each day. During a typical strings class, he will begin by having the students play scales for intonation, quality of sound, and technique. Most of the period will be devoted to working on problems with current pieces, with some time devoted to sight reading and the teaching of musical terms, abbreviations, and signs.

The day is long for a high school music teacher. Four days a week, Thomas supervises rehearsals of different sections of the orchestra after school; every Tuesday evening he holds a three-hour rehearsal of performance and possible contest pieces to discover problems that the students can work on at home and in their sections. Thomas receives a stipend for the work he does with students beyond the regular school day, as most high school music teachers do.

During the school year, he will be the guest conductor for junior and senior high school orchestras and act as a judge at several music contests. He also finds time to serve on the board of the state school music association. In the summer, Thomas will often act as the orchestra director of a summer music camp. Today, when this busy music teacher has time, he sings in a church choir. During his teaching career, he has also at various times played the cello with different symphony groups and directed choirs.

Thomas's goal is to give his students a good experience in his orchestra classes, which he hopes will lead to a lifetime of enjoying good music and the playing of a musical instrument. He sees himself as being a student-oriented music teacher rather than a performance-oriented teacher. Because he is so sensitive to the needs of his students, the walls of his office abound with plaques and letters of appreciation, like the following one from his orchestra students when he left that school for his present position.

A Tribute to the Conductor

As our teacher, we have both loved and admired him, for he has been much more than a simple instructor. Not only has he been the key to our musical growth, but he has been our friend and our inspiration as well. Through him we have been encouraged to better ourselves both with music and in our daily lives.

As our conductor, he has shared with us his wonderful gift of music. Through his help and guidance we have each been allowed to develop our inner talents into a product that we can use to bring joy to others.

Teaching in a College

Martin Marks dreamed of being a performer as a child—a dream he realized by playing the piano with symphony orchestras and giving solo recitals in the Midwest. Besides performing, he also gave piano lessons to as many as one hundred students a week, plus studying for his bachelor's and master's degrees in music with a performance orientation. His outstanding reputation as a teacher and pianist led to his appointment as a part-time and then a full-time professor of music. Today, his schedule includes giving classes in piano literature and performance anxiety as well as teaching piano to college students and a few private students.

Private Music Instruction

Being a private music teacher is an excellent way to combine teaching and a love of music. Working in their homes, students' homes, and studios, these teachers usually instruct school-aged children. The number of students depends on the local demand as well as the individual's reputation as a skilled teacher. Since most of their students are in school during the day, a private teacher's day does not normally begin until school is over.

Fees

Fees usually range from $10 to $20 per lesson, although some experts command fees as high as $150 per lesson. What you earn depends greatly on your reputation as well as the demand for music instruction in your area.

A Private Teacher

With an educational background of a bachelor's degree in music education with a minor in music therapy and a master's in performance, Melissa Williams has taught music in elementary school and worked at a residential treatment center for emotionally disturbed children. Today, she teaches tuba, euphonium, and trombone to about forty students, plays in symphony orchestras in two cities, and does some freelancing at recording studios. To get started as a private teacher in a new city, she joined a brass choir and played with a local symphony, where she met many school music teachers who have recommended her to students in their classes. In her free time Melissa practices the tuba, hoping to win an audition to be a regular in a major symphony orchestra. To hone her skills, this accomplished musician takes lessons from an expert player with the Chicago Symphony.

Music Therapists—Helping People Through Music

Music therapists are a bold, aggressive group who are pounding on doors of hospitals and other treatment centers, explaining how adding a music therapist would enhance the facility. Although people have been helped by music through the ages, it is only since the 1950s that music therapists have been slowly accepted by the medical profession as a part of its treatment team. The American Music Therapy Association describes music therapy as the use of music in the accomplishment of therapeutic aims: the restoration, maintenance, and improvement of mental and physical health.

As a result of their efforts, music therapists are now being added to the staffs at some hospices, nursing homes, rehabilitation centers, prisons, school systems, clinics, and day care and treatment centers for children. At the same time, due to current budget restraints, many music therapists are being forced to take jobs with titles like activity or program director—which means that music is only a small part of their jobs.

Music therapists do not just work in institutions. Freelance music therapists continue working with patients who have been discharged from a hospital, easing the adjustment back into the community. Therapists also work in their studios with young children and adults who have been referred to them by health professionals.

As members of a treatment team, music therapists work with doctors, social workers, occupational therapists, nurses, and psychologists. As individuals, the team members meet with new patients and assess how their disciplines can help these people. Then the team meets and discusses the role each discipline will play in helping in the patient's recovery and sets goals for the treatment plan. The committee will meet again every few months to review each patient's progress. The music therapist will use music and music activities usually in a group setting to bring about desirable changes in behavior. Since music has a great effect on people's feelings and emotions, it helps the patients share their thoughts with others in a nonthreatening manner.

Qualifications

Music therapists need to be emotionally stable individuals who can work well with both their clients and the personnel of the therapeutic treatment team. They will also find it helpful to be able to play more than one musical instrument. To become a music therapist, a bachelor's degree in music therapy with courses in music, music therapy, psychology, and the social sciences, followed by a six-month internship at an approved treatment facility, is required. After completing the degree program or equivalent and an internship, a music therapist can apply to become a Registered Music Therapist with the American Music Therapy Association. Registration shows that he or she has met the organization's rigorous educational and clinical training standards. To become board certified, music therapists must take a national music therapy examination that is recognized by the National Commission on Certifying Agencies. This ensures that board certified music therapists have the highest professional qualifications.

Salaries

The salary range for jobs as music therapists is from below $20,000 to slightly more than $40,000 a year. According to the American Music Therapy Association, the average salary for full-time music therapists working in the following areas were

nursing homes	$29,434
physical rehabilitation	$31,747
in-patient psychiatric units	$33,540
adult day care	$32,968
K–12 schools	$34,993
corrections	$38,824

Benefits will vary greatly depending on the facility where a therapist works. Many jobs in state and federal facilities offer the benefits of civil service positions.

For More Information

The American Music Therapy Association has more information on becoming a music therapist, including a list of the colleges and universities that have degree programs in the field. You can visit the Web site at http://www.musictherapy.org or write to the American Music Therapy Association, 8455 Colesville Road, Suite 1000, Silver Spring, MD 20910.

A Music Therapist's Job

After learning more about music therapy, Barbara Romerhaus switched her major from music education to music therapy because she enjoyed helping people and liked working in hospital treatment facilities. She concentrated on piano and flute in college, but then learned to play the Autoharp and different percussion, string, and woodwind instruments in order to be able to help future patients using a variety of instruments.

Barbara's first job was as acting director of music therapy at a state hospital. She could not be appointed director because the facility required two years of experience for appointment to this position. Barbara worked a forty-hour week setting up patient choir groups, teaching musical skills groups, and helping patients tap into community resources when they left the hospital. It is an important part of the job for music therapists to find community music groups where discharged patients can go to continue their music interests.

Barbara's next job was on a research project in a psychiatric hospital, doing a study of autistic children under the guidelines of a major university. Like all research studies, the program was very structured and research oriented. Barbara worked with ten autistic children, teaching them various motor skills, concepts like "up and down" and "right and left," and even numbers and letters—through music and song. According to Barbara, music helps people learn and remember information better than any other medium because of the structure within it. Music was also used as positive reinforcement toward attaining a desired behavior change. The autistic children responded positively to the music and were rewarded by being able to listen to favorite songs. Some of the children had language skills, while others let Barbara know their musical preferences through body language.

After two years with the research program, Barbara became the director of the hospital's adult music therapy program for the adult psychiatric program. Her duties were quite similar to those of her first job at a state hospital. She conducted classes in such areas as music and relaxation, music and movement to help increase the patients' energy and motivation, and music and recreation to help patients acquire leisure skills.

After an eleven-year break in her career path to raise a family, Barbara returned to music therapy at a state hospital—illustrating that a career in this profession can be resumed after even a break of more than a decade. She became the rehabilitation therapy supervisor at the hospital with twelve people under her supervision, including two music therapists, two occupational therapists, a recreational therapist, and therapy assistants. Her duties included administering, planning, and making sure that the programs her staff members were conducting met the needs of the patients. She also had to make sure her staff worked within the allotted budget, and she attended hospital administrators' meetings. In addition, she was in charge of the music therapy internship program at her facility.

Music Librarians

Libraries with large collections of music books, recordings, musical scores, and periodicals associated with music have jobs for music librarians. The focus of music collections in public libraries is usually general, with materials ranging from popular to classical music. Some libraries, like the Library of Congress and the New York Public Library, have so much information about music that they serve as research centers. Academic libraries have more scholarly materials than most public libraries, and some will specialize in a particular area, like the jazz library at Rutgers University. Music librarians can also find jobs at places that have large music collections that need to be kept in order—such as radio and television stations, large music publishers, and professional music associations.

Most music libraries are quite small and specialized, so music librarians typically have to perform a variety of tasks, from dealing with patrons to handling administrative duties. Library patrons can add great interest to this job as you may work with young music students, music teachers, professional artists, and researchers. In this job, you are most likely to work at a large university or in a large city. Because the field is so small, there is limited opportunity for advancement.

It is not easy to become a music librarian. Most music librarians have master's degrees in library science from an accredited program of the American Library Association. For many positions, they are also required to have master's or even Ph.D. degrees in some aspect of music.

Nevertheless, music lovers do not have to have advanced degrees to work in music libraries, as there are jobs there for clerks who usually have completed technical or associate degrees in library science. However, almost everyone working in music libraries will work with library clients, so skill in interacting with people is another job requirement.

Salaries
Music librarians who work in public or university libraries will earn the same salaries as other librarians. The average salary of these librarians is about $35,800 a year, while beginning

librarians with master's degrees and no experience will earn approximately $28,700 a year. Music librarians who work in special libraries will earn slightly more money.

A Music Librarian

Equipped with a bachelor's degree in music education, Anna Thompson spent three years teaching music before returning to college to earn a master's degree in library science. She obtained her job as a music librarian in a major Midwest city through an interview held at her college. Because the music library was large, the music librarians specialized. Anna was in charge of all the sound recordings and cassette tapes, and she made selections of scores to be added to the band and ensemble sections. Part of her duties consisted of developing educational programs for the general public and the schools. For example, she organized a series of woodwind recitals. This task required her to compile a bibliography, select performers, finalize contracts with them, and handle the publicity for the event.

Most professions have associations that allow members to extend their knowledge of the profession and to network with others in the field. Anna found further satisfaction in her career by being very active in the Music Library Association. She chaired the public library committee and served as chair for local arrangements when the association met in her city.

Symphony Orchestras

When the conductors of the more than fifteen hundred symphony orchestras in the United States raise their batons to begin a performance, there are always people behind the scenes seeing to the orchestra's management. The larger a symphony is, the greater the number of people required to handle such administrative tasks as raising funds, marketing, publicizing the group, negotiating contracts, and handling the finances. Although jobs with these orchestras are very appealing to music lovers, the number of jobs is definitely limited: there are only thirty major symphony orchestras in the United States. Job titles and responsibilities will vary depending on the orchestra; however, music lovers are likely to find the following or similar administrative positions with major orchestras.

MANAGING DIRECTOR   has responsibility for all aspects of operating an orchestra and must implement policies of the symphony board.

OPERATIONS MANAGER   assists the managing director in the operation of the orchestra.

DIRECTOR OF DEVELOPMENT   is in charge of all fund-raising programs.

BUSINESS MANAGER   handles all financial matters.

PUBLICITY DIRECTOR   deals with the press and manages all aspects of promoting an orchestra.

DIRECTOR OF EDUCATION   works with schools in developing concerts and other educational activities.

TICKET SERVICE DIRECTOR   is in charge of the sale of tickets.

Besides these top management positions, music lovers can find at least seventy more jobs at major orchestras as part of the administrative staff. Fewer jobs will be available at medium-sized orchestras, while smaller orchestras may employ only a manager who is assisted by volunteers. Community orchestras may just employ a part-time manager or be completely run by volunteers.

Symphony orchestras hiring administrative staff look for individuals who have a background in music coupled with bachelor's or master's degrees in business or arts administration. Music lovers who want to work in this area will find it easier to get jobs if they have worked with a symphony as a volunteer or intern.

Working as Director of Development

Raising money is never an easy job, but that is the number one responsibility of directors of development for symphony orchestras. They plan, coordinate, and implement all fund-raising programs. Sponsoring cocktail parties, gala dinners, symphony balls, and other special events are some of the ways that directors of development raise funds. They may also initiate direct mail campaigns and telethons as money raisers. Time must also be spent searching and applying for business and government grants. Since volunteers play such an important role in soliciting funds, development directors must devise programs to recognize their invaluable help. Part of the director's job is to approve all newsletters, news releases, and fund-raising literature. And the director must also supervise staff and run the department within the budget.

The secret to success in this position is in producing results— successfully raising money. You will need to be an enthusiastic and persuasive individual to bring in donors. In order to advance, many directors move to larger and more prestigious symphony orchestras.

Salaries

What you will earn as a director depends on the size of the orchestra. A small orchestra may only offer $12,000 a year, while larger orchestras will pay $60,000 and up per year.

A Vice President of Development

The Indianapolis Symphony Orchestra (ISO) is one the nation's few full-time, fifty-two-week-season orchestras. As vice president of development, Tuck Shulhof is responsible for the fund-raising programs that are necessary to the financial stability of the Orchestra and that include the annual operating fund and the Orchestra's endowment. In addition to a broad range of music performances, the Orchestra's music education programs, particularly for children, play a role in fund-raising. When he contacts corporations and foundations, he explains the added value the Orchestra brings to the community and its quality of life.

On a typical day, Tuck will devote his time to a wide range of activities. In addition to some management responsibilities, time is devoted to identifying companies and foundations that are potential sponsors of various classical and pops concert series and the Orchestra's twenty-five education programs. After identifying the interests of the potential sponsors, he and his staff customize proposals for sponsorships. There are meetings with his staff and organizations as well as a continual barrage of phone conversations with volunteers and donors. Tuck sees his position as essentially one of marketing the opportunities for corporations and other organizations and donors to identify themselves with the Orchestra, its performances, and its programs.

Career Path

Unlike many others who direct the fund-raising activities of symphony orchestras, Tuck did not work in development earlier. Instead, he came to this position after retiring from a thirty-year career in corporate and government affairs and corporate law. Tuck was offered his present job because he had been long involved in corporate philanthropy and in volunteer activities with the Orchestra and other not-for-profit organizations.

Entry-Level Positions in Development

Large symphony orchestras frequently have internship and summer positions that give a bird's-eye view of what working in development is like. These positions usually involve working on small projects and help individuals gain valuable work experience. Before applying for an entry-level position in development, you should have a college degree and some fund-raising experience. A few schools have degrees in arts administration or management, which is the preferred degree for this job. If this is not possible, applicants should have course work in marketing, public relations, and business.

On the job, entry-level workers in development are typically assigned tasks associated with donors. They will plan events for donors and accommodate their needs for tickets. If their work is effective, they will be on the path to upward mobility in this career.

Publicity Director

While the musicians are busy playing and the director of development is trying to raise funds, the publicity director is telling the media about the orchestra and promoting future symphony performances. Newspapers, magazines, radio stations, and television stations have to be notified about special events such as children's concerts and holiday specials. Stories must be followed up so that the director or one of the staff members can see if additional interviews or photos are needed.

Salaries

Individuals working as publicity directors will typically receive salaries in the $30,000 range. The size of the orchestra will influence how much a public relations specialist earns.

A Media Relations Manager

At the Indianapolis Symphony Orchestra, the position of publicity director is called media relations manager. For the past nine years, this job has been held by Tim Northcutt. He is a music lover—an absolute requirement for this position. Tim can still recall the incredible experience that he had attending his first lollipop concert (a symphony program for children). His love of music continued in college, where his roommates were music majors and he became hooked on opera.

Courses in journalism and political science helped Tim obtain his first job in public relations, working as media secretary for a congressional candidate during his senior year in college. Successful work on this campaign led to stints as a reporter covering the Indiana General Assembly and campaign jobs for governors, senators, mayors, and congressional representatives in Kansas, California, Texas, Minnesota, Arizona, and Florida.

Desiring to stay in one place after marriage, Tim accepted a job at the Tampa Bay Performing Arts Center, a huge $57 million complex that holds more than eight hundred performances a year within its three theaters. At the center, Tim dealt with all kinds of entertainers, from comedians to opera stars. The center wanted Tim for this position because of his media background in dealing with *Time*, *Newsweek*, the Washington press corps, and major television networks during political campaigns. Tim wanted the job because of his love of culture and saw it as an opportunity to create a better understanding of the arts.

In his current position as media relations manager for the Indianapolis Symphony Orchestra, Tim handles media relations with the local, regional, national, and international press, along with telling the ISO story to the public. While the administrative side of the symphony operates like a typical corporation, the organization is quite innovative on its artistic and programming side. For example, the orchestra holds the Symphony Promenade, which is a spring festival of thematic classical music, and Symphony on the Prairie, where people relax on the ground with a picnic and enjoy the music. There is also the Ameritech's Yuletide Celebration. ISO was the first orchestra in North America to do a multidiscipline holiday show. Tim handles the publicity for all of these events. He looks forward to coming to work each day because there are always new challenges in his job.

Performance Librarian—a Job with Music

While an administrative job supports the functioning of a symphony orchestra, the job of performance librarian involves working closely with the orchestra and the music. These librarians' comprehensive knowledge of music, combined with their library skills, helps them get music to the musicians. First, they obtain the music from the orchestra's library or buy or rent new music. Rented music must then be returned when the orchestra is no longer using it. Once the music is obtained, the performance librarian is responsible for getting the music ready for the orchestra by adding the bowings and all the different marks that will be necessary. Often the librarian works with the conductor and soloists in the preparation of the music. The librarian must also attend all rehearsals and concerts at home and on tour to make sure that the music is handed out to each musician and then collected after each performance. This is definitely not a job with regular hours such as music librarians in libraries have.

The number of jobs is obviously limited by the number of orchestras requiring this service. In smaller orchestras this job is handled part-time by one of the musicians. Most performance librarians are current or former musicians from the orchestra who through courses have gained their library experience.

Salaries

Pay for this position varies and depends greatly upon whether the librarian is also considered a member of the orchestra eligible for union benefits. Jobs with the major orchestras that perform year-round vary from $50,000 to $80,000 a year. Individuals with other orchestras that have a shorter performing season will earn less.

Performance Librarian for a Major Orchestra

Michael Runyon is the performance librarian for the Indianapolis Symphony Orchestra. He began playing the piano in first grade and later picked up the trumpet, French horn, and harmonica. During his high school years, he became interested in composition and began composing and arranging for the school swing choir and jazz band. He went on to study composition in college and says that most college programs allow the study of both classical composition—for symphonies, ballets, and operas—and commercial composition—for jingles, film scores, and television shows. His love is classical composition. Throughout his college years, Michael worked as a copyist, arranger, and studio musician; he also played in bands, taught at universities, worked in art groups, and wrote grants. Michael holds bachelor's, master's, and a doctorate degrees in composition. Because of his musical background, he can customize parts for the orchestra and analyze scores for them.

Michael, with the help of one full-time and two part-time performance librarians, gets the parts ready for the individual symphony players. When the orchestra buys or rents music, it is never ready for the musicians' stands as it comes out of the package. Often the music has been written for more or fewer instruments than the Indianapolis Symphony has. Then decisions have to be made whether additional musicians will be brought in, whether some musicians will be allowed to go on holiday, or whether some musicians will be assigned extra parts. The principals of each section and the conductor mark the music to indicate changes so that everyone in each section will be reading the same music. Michael and the other performance librarians see that these changes are made for each musician.

As a performance librarian, Michael needs to be preparing music years in advance of its presentation as well as honing details for compositions soon to be performed. His duties also extend to working on cost analysis of proposed concerts and answering questions such as how many musicians will be needed and whether soloists will be required. Michael likes working with the production of a concert. He is able to handle the pressure of having the music be perfect for each musician when the conductor raises his baton. During symphony performances, Michael prefers to just sit out front and enjoy the music as a consumer rather than as a producer, because he has done his part to make the music ready for the musicians.

Opera—Acting, Singing, and Music

Opera is a drama that brings music lovers beautiful music sung by sumptuous voices in elaborate settings. Because opera requires so many singers and musicians for a performance, it is very expensive to stage. The major problem of all opera companies is securing sufficient funds. In the United States, the most famous company is the Metropolitan Opera in New York, which also has the New York City Opera. San Francisco, Boston, Chicago, and Santa Fe, New Mexico, also have important opera companies. While many other cities have opera companies, they generally have short seasons and are likely to perform just a few operas.

Even though an opera audience will only see the performers on stage, the orchestra, and the conductor, a large group of people is required behind the scenes to stage these complicated performances. Major opera companies will have permanent organizations with general managers, music directors, stage directors, costume and set designers, administrative staff, technical staff (electricians and sound engineers), wardrobe handlers, and stagehands. However, many companies will only have a small permanent administrative staff. Because there are few opera companies with year-round staffs, there is a limited opportunity for opera lovers to find employment—although there is always a need for outstanding fund-raisers and volunteers.

Director of San Francisco Opera Center

Outside of New York City, the opera company that gives the greatest number of performances is the San Francisco Opera. An important part of the success of the company lies in the San Francisco Opera Center. Its mandate is to educate and train singers, pianists, and technicians (stage crew) so that they can become either part of the San Francisco Opera or pursue other operatic options. As director of the opera center, Richard Harrell produces operas that allow these young professionals to train by performing. For each opera, he has the responsibility of choosing a conductor, director, and set and costume designers as well as putting the singers in the right parts. Besides managing all training programs, Richard serves as an acting coach and director. In addition, he assists in raising funds to support the activities of the opera center.

Career Path

Richard has always worked in the theater. He has been an opera singer, stagehand, teacher, stage director, and producer, and he created his own performing arts festival. After receiving a bachelor's degree in vocal performance, he worked for fifteen years as a professional singer. Richard was always interested in teaching acting and directing and was hired as a stage director and teacher for opera while he sang professionally. Eventually, he returned to school and received a master of fine arts degree in stage direction for opera. He served on the faculty of the Juilliard School and ultimately became the director of the opera department at Juilliard. After several years, he moved to San Francisco to become the director of the San Francisco Opera Center.

Career Advice

If you want to have a job like his, Richard says that you must have a passionate interest in the arts and a desire to explore all facets that converge in the opera world.

The Publishing Side of Music

Adding to the diversity of jobs in the music world is the publishing side of music—including the publication of books and magazines on music, instruction books for different instruments, sheet music, and school textbooks. Music lovers who want to work in the book and magazine side of publishing need to couple a knowledge of music with writing skills. There are magazines for almost every musical interest, so music lovers have the opportunity to spend their days writing about their favorite form of music whether it is classical, country, opera, or heavy metal.

Publishing Sheet Music

Every piece of sheet music that musicians use has been published by a music publishing company. There are large publishing houses as well as small, independent music publishers. Many individuals start out with large companies and then leave these companies to start their own firms. Other publishing houses are launched by writers of hit tunes to sell their own music.

No matter what their size, music publishing companies, large and small, must select music that will sell. This is an important knack that determines how successful a company will be. One hit popular song can make a very large amount of money for a music publisher. Once a publishing company decides that a piece of music is salable, contracts are negotiated with the writer and the material is copyrighted. The music is put in the right form for printing and then distributed.

A Sheet Music Publisher

Scott Houston and his father have found a unique marketing niche in the music publishing business. They are educational music publishers who sell band and choir arrangements for use in schools, instructional books for music instruments, and manuscript paper. Their three-year-old firm has four employees. Scott has the responsibility of evaluating submissions from personal acquaintances and other people who know what type of music the company publishes. He contacts the writers of salable music and offers them standard royalty contracts. Next, the company obtains the copyright for the music. Then the music is sent out to a music engraving company, which prepares the piece for printing. Scott does the layout and the pre-press production work, and the music is printed in-house. For sixteen weeks of the year, Scott and his father are on the road separately, going to conventions and visiting stores so retailers will know their products.

Music Copyists—Preparing Sheet Music for Publication

Music copyists transcribe each individual musical part from a score onto paper. For example, a copyist will go through a complete score and write out the entire part for the flute, making it much easier for the flutist to play the part. Traditionally, copying has been done with a special technical pen, with the same process followed for each musical instrument. Just as the computer has changed other areas, it has revolutionized copying music. Copyists can now play on a keyboard directly into a computer. The information is then translated into printed notations. This is a very quick process, and, with the aid of a modem, copyists can quickly send completed scores anywhere in the world to music publishers and other groups needing their work. Most copyists will either own their own businesses or work for music publishers.

Blue Note Engraving

In their free time, Jeff Wiedenfeld and his wife Julie run Blue Note Engraving, a company that copies music. Their company is fully computerized, and the speed of the computer is very important in getting music to the clients on time. According to Jeff, the computer does it all. Publishing houses, music groups, and composers need copies quickly, and with the modem he can get copy to a publisher—even one in London—without much delay. Julie and Jeff do no copying by hand because they have instructed the computer to do it all. Although their business is based in the Midwest, they have clients throughout the country.

Publishing School Music Textbooks

School children do not just use textbooks for mathematics, history, and reading; they also use textbooks in their music classes. This is a specialized industry within music publishing because of the need to meet age-specific learning requirements.

A Music Textbook Publisher

Larry Hillman is the executive editor for music at Silver Burdette and Ginn. In this position, he is responsible for both creating the company's music materials for kindergarten through eighth grade and for supervising a staff of fourteen editors—all of whom are musicians and former music teachers. As part of his job, Larry speaks with both teachers and students to determine what type of product each grade level needs. Dreaming up the product is the creative side of his job. The administrative side includes supervising his department, making business projections, overseeing the budget, and dealing with sales and marketing. An appealing aspect of this job for Larry is being in direct daily contact with music, since he supervises the recording of every song used in the series.

Career Path

In studying Larry's career path to his present job, music lovers can see other job opportunities they might like to explore. Larry's first job was as a music teacher. His qualifications for this job included playing the piano and organ since he was in second grade and holding both bachelor's and master's degrees in music. He also had a minor in business, which turned out to be very helpful in his career. After teaching music from kindergarten through junior college for ten years, Larry became a music consultant with Silver Burdette; this was both a sales and service job. He would present the company's products to the teachers and then go back and help the teachers learn to use the materials after a school had purchased them. Larry was next promoted to product manager of music, essentially a marketing job. He had to come up with advertising campaigns and help oversee research and product development. Before becoming executive editor, Larry was a program editor who had supervising responsibilities and did direct editing of music materials.

The Recording Industry

The recording side of music represents a multibillion dollar industry that produces all the cassettes, CDs, tapes, and records music lovers buy in order to listen to their beloved music. Today, there are more than two thousand companies producing and selling music—which adds up to a considerable number of jobs for music lovers. There are giant corporations, such as CBS, Sony, RCA, Warner, MCA, and Polygram, which produce almost every type of music and have a large stable of artists. On the other hand, there are very small companies that may only produce one type of music or the music of a few artists. The three leading cities for recording music are New York, Los Angeles, and Nashville, although companies are scattered throughout the United States. The largest companies will have offices in several cities. Most no longer have recording studios, assigning this work to small studios close to the artists or their companies.

The making and selling of a recording, whether it is a cassette, tape, or CD, is a complicated process. At the giant corporations, individuals work in a specific area such as promotion, marketing, sales, or publicity; at smaller companies, employees tend to have their hands in almost every aspect of producing and selling a recording. What follows is a description of the people who are involved in producing a recording and exactly what their roles are so that music lovers can see what jobs might appeal to them in the recording arena.

Artist and Repertoire Department (A&R)

This is the group that finds talent as well as the music an artist or group will perform. The music may come from a staff writer, the artist or group, a new arrangement of an old favorite, or a demo sent to the company. A&R works with the producer in planning all the details of the recording, from the number of musicians to choosing a recording studio. A&R is also in charge of the budget for a recording, which includes paying the bills and keeping financial records. In reality, A&R seems to be in on almost every decision about a recording. The department works with advertising, promotion, public relations, and marketing to determine the game plan for releasing a recording.

Art Department

The design of album, tape, and cassette covers plays an important role in the selling of recordings. Designers, graphic artists, and photographers work on their creation.

Promotion, Publicity, and Advertising

A well-integrated plan has to be developed to catch the eyes and ears of the prospective buyers of recordings. The greater the audience who reads, listens to, or hears about a new recording, the greater the chance it will be successful. This means getting radio stations to play the recording and talk show personalities and music critics to interview the artist or group, scheduling television appearances and press conferences, and buying advertisements in all the media. It may even include coming up with a gimmick such as a special T-shirt, pin, or hat.

Sales and Marketing

Marketing strategies have to be developed to get recordings into the hands of the consumer. This involves close work with promotion, publicity, and advertising as well as setting up displays in stores and visiting or calling stores, music directors at radio and television stations, and music columnists at newspapers and magazines.

Music lovers desiring to work for large recording companies will find having a degree in some field of business or music business helpful in securing a job. Working as an intern or in an entry-level position can give job seekers the experience most recording companies expect them to have. Jobs can be learned about through contacts in the field and ads in newspapers and trade papers like *Billboard* and *Cashbox*.

Recording Studios and Recording Engineers

It has been said that there is a recording studio on almost every corner in Nashville. Recent advances in technology have made it possible for small studios to produce excellent sound recordings. Today, music is often recorded at certain studios because of the expertise of the recording engineers who work at, use, or own these studios. No matter how excellent an artist, act, or the personnel at a recording company are, the success of a recording also depends on the end product the recording engineer creates.

Recording engineers operate the sophisticated equipment used to make recordings. Their job begins with the setting up of the equipment for a recording session to produce the sound they want. During the actual recording session, they must push the right buttons and switches to get the desired sound. Finally, and this requires considerable skill, they must mix the recorded tracks down to either two or four tracks. At times, a recording is made at several studios—even in different cities. For example, the rhythm bed may be laid down in one studio and the vocals at another while the sound is mixed at yet another studio.

Some recording engineers hold bachelor's degrees in electrical engineering. Others may have completed courses at vocational technical schools, and some learn by serving as apprentices. There is a great deal of competition for positions as recording engineers. One of the best ways to secure a job is by serving as an intern. Although recording engineers may begin by earning no more than minimum wage, successful engineers working for name performers or groups can easily make $100,000 a year.

Aire Born

Mike Wilson and John Bolt are partners who own Aire Born, a recording studio located in the Midwest. They rent studio time plus their expertise as recording engineers. The two have created a successful business recording commercials, albums, and corporate materials. More than 50 percent of their work comes from servicing a small niche in the recording business—music publishers. These clients want recordings to demonstrate the sound of their sheet music to potential customers.

Mike and John traveled slightly different paths in becoming recording engineers, although both feel they gained their expertise through hands-on work experience. Mike obtained a degree in music business and went to a recording workshop during college. While in high school and later on, he played in a rock band that had its own eight-track recording studio, which gave him practical experience in sound recording.

John, on the other hand, went to a technical school as a part of high school and took a course in sound engineering. After high school, he also attended a recording workshop. The workshop then offered him a job that gave John his work experience in the business. In his next job, he worked at a studio owned by a sacred music writer and demonstrated his expertise by making three gold records in the religious market. Mike and John met while working at different studios and quickly found that they shared similar values as well as the goal of owning a twenty-four track recording studio. They decided to mortgage their homes and start Aire Born, which has proved to be a successful venture.

The Bengemark for Music

Johann Sebastian Bach wrote music to order for patrons. In the same way, Doug Benge, owner of The Bengemark for Music, creates music for clients, usually advertisers and businesses seeking music for meetings and new product launches. The first step involves talking to the client to find out what the music is to accomplish—the desired image or mood. Then Doug will use a computer program as he composes a piece of music with or without words. The musical notation program transmits what he plays on a keyboard to notes he can see on the computer screen. He removes the floppy disk from the computer, goes into his recording studio, puts the disk into a computer, and assigns the newly composed piece to different synthesizers using two software programs to create the music in a rough form. The client listens to the music, and any necessary changes are made before the final product is recorded.

Composing has certainly changed since Bach's time. Like Bach, this modern composer is a musician who shares a great love of music. Doug has an impressive academic background, with a bachelor's degree in philosophy and a master's in English. His music background includes playing in bands.

The Retail Side of Music

Music lovers are good customers of retail stores selling records, tapes, CDs, sheet music, and musical instruments. These stores can also be pleasant places for them to work, with music frequently drifting through the air plus customers who share the music lover's interest in music, leading to many congenial conversations on different aspects of music.

Owners and managers of retail music and record stores must have a solid knowledge of music as well as of business. While a

college education is not required, courses at this level can provide a good background in both music and business. Salespersons
need to be knowledgeable about music and skilled in dealing
with customers. If they work in a store selling instruments, it is a
decided plus for them to be able to play one or more instruments.
Being a salesperson is a good way to enter the retail side of music.
With experience, salespersons can advance to managerial positions or even to owning their own stores.

Owner and Manager of a Music Store

Franklin W. Penwell owns and manages Frank's Fiddle Shop in
Indianapolis, which sells, rents, restores, and repairs string
instruments. Originally, Franklin was a bassist playing classical
music in a small symphony orchestra as well as jazz on weekends.
His main job, however, was teaching music in a public school. He
soon observed that his students were having problems getting
their instruments repaired satisfactorily and back on time, so
Franklin taught himself how to repair string instruments through
reading books and trial and error. After a while, he was not only
repairing his students' instruments but also the instruments of
students from other schools. The success of his repair business,
which he was operating out of a two-car garage, led Franklin to
start his present business.

Today, Frank's Fiddle Shop has five employees—a bookkeeper
and four others who work in the store as well as give lessons on
string instruments and help Franklin repair instruments, mostly
bows. Franklin himself does most of the repair work as well as
overseeing the business side of the firm.

Career Advice

If you are interested in a career in repairing instruments,
Franklin points out that you will typically learn this skill on the
job. There are also a few schools that teach this specialized art.

Glamour Jobs in Music

You can combine your love of music with a glamorous career in the limelight or behind the scenes when you have a job in radio, television, and movies or with rising stars and superstars. Perhaps you could be one of the many people in the background helping famous musicians like pop star Madonna or violinist Isaac Stern perform. On the other hand, you can grab part of the limelight for yourself with a job as a personality playing music from country to classical on radio or commenting on operas and symphonies to radio and television audiences or even introducing music videos to MTV viewers.

Radio and Music

Wake up in the morning to the sound of music drifting from your clock radio. Hop in the car and drive with music easing the boredom. Jog along a path with music from the radio setting the rhythm of your stride. Wherever people go, their radios go with them, and, much of the time, the radios are tuned to music programs. Depending on the organization of a radio station, the individual selecting the music can be the program director, the music director, the on-air personality, or someone holding some combination of these titles. No particular educational requirements exist for these jobs; however, knowledge of music is definitely a prerequisite. Most people currently working at these positions began their careers in small radio stations working at any job they could find or through a college internship. The typical career ladder is from on-air personality position (also called disc jockey) to music director to program director and from small station to larger station at every job change.

Salaries

The pay for being an on-air personality in a major market can be quite good; the average income for this position is currently

$105,000 a year, with some earning several million. Pay is even good in smaller markets, ranging from $30,000 to $50,000 a year.

Morning Personality

Scott Fischer is the morning personality of WENS, working the 6 A.M. to 10 A.M. shift at this all-music radio station in Indianapolis. For thirty-two years, Scott has worked as an on-air personality. Sometimes he cannot believe that he is paid to have such fun in the morning.

Music has always played an important role in this music lover's life. As a child, Scott collected and listened to records, besides playing the mellophone and French horn. It seemed natural for him to select a career that combined music with his other love— radio. At college, Scott majored in theater and communications, a useful background for individuals seeking employment in radio. However, Scott really got his first exposure to the radio business in college by working at the campus radio station and a local radio station on weekends and during the summer. After graduation, Scott spent several months scouring the smaller radio markets for a job as a disc jockey personality, sending his resume and demo tape to stations. While most on-air personalities begin their careers at small market stations working for salaries close to minimum wage, Scott secured a job in a medium market station in Des Moines. From Des Moines, he went to Denver to work as on-air personality and music director for more money and at a better time slot—the typical career path for on-air personalities. After Denver, Scott worked in major radio market stations in Chicago and Atlanta before securing his present job in Indianapolis.

On-Air Personality and Music Director

J. D. Cannon of WFMS in Indianapolis, a country radio station, was given the Large Market Personality of the Year award in 1998 by the Country Music Association. He prepared for his career as an on-air personality by attending a vocational/

technical school and studying broadcasting for a year. Part of the curriculum at the school was technical training, and part was announcing. J. D. learned of his first job from another student at the school who told him about an ad for an afternoon news anchor at a Madison, Wisconsin, radio station. From this job, J. D. went on to become an on-air personality at the station.

In his current job, J. D. is also the music director, a position that requires the ability to judge and predict which new songs will become popular with listeners. Each week, J. D. has to sift through approximately fifty new songs to select the four or five that will be added to the rotation at his station. This is a time-consuming job that begins on Monday, when he spends two or three hours on the phone talking to promoters. On Tuesday, he enters all the music into the computer to create the computer-generated play list for the week. Songs have to be categorized by J. D. according to current popularity so the computer program can create the printed list detailing when and how often songs will be played. J. D. uses information from research companies, music charts, and publications such as *Radio and Records*, *Billboard*, and the *Gavin Report* to determine which songs are hot locally and which songs are starting to lose popular appeal. On Wednesday, he listens to all the new products and decides which ones to insert in his previously adjusted computer list.

Because J. D. is an on-air personality, he must also spend time each day preparing for his daily program, which includes chitchat about music and information on artists and concerts between segments of nonstop music. In addition, he spends time making commercials for the program. Away from the radio station, J. D., like other on-air personalities, spends considerable time doing personal appearance work at parades and shopping malls.

Program Director

Ed Lennon held a wide variety of jobs—from selling cars to owning a fire alarm company—before he began working in radio part-time selling ads. Quickly, the radio bug bit, and Ed found he was spending more time at the station fooling with the equipment and writing and producing commercials than selling ads. His next job was as a part-time producer of a radio show at another station. He proved himself by working forty- and fifty-hour weeks at his part-time job. Soon he was pushing the buttons and cuing up the records for Dick Clark's syndicated show.

At every opportunity, Ed always volunteered and took on more responsibility, which led to a temporary full-time position producing commercials and then to the job of production director responsible for the production of all commercials and promotions at the station. Being willing to work hard throughout his entire career helped Ed obtain a job as program manager for WIBC—a large station in a major market area where he supervised the on-air staff and directed the on-air sound, which included choosing the right music for WIBC's audiences.

A Music Critic

Imagine the satisfaction for a music lover of being involved vicariously with music through writing about concerts, reviewing records and CDs, and interviewing music presenters and musicians. This is the job that Jay Harvey had as a classical and jazz music critic for the *Indianapolis Star*, and it seems like almost a perfect job for music lovers. With a background of trombone playing, a bachelor's degree in English, and a master's in teaching, Jay entered the teaching profession. After a few years, he decided on a different career path and went into newspaper work. For fifteen years, he reviewed classical music, visual arts programs, and some theater productions for the *Flint Journal* in Michigan, as well as writing book reviews and general features for the paper. Wishing to concentrate on music, Jay moved to his current paper as a music critic.

A typical workday, which began at 2 P.M., might involve writing a review of *Porgy and Bess*, which he saw the previous evening; completing a piece on the labor and management problems of the local symphony orchestra; listening to recordings sent to him to review; and writing short announcements about music activities throughout the state. During a usual work week, Jay would attend three or four musical performances, illustrating the varying days and hours that music critics work. Job requirements for the position of music critic on a newspaper include having a good ear and an excellent knowledge of music plus good writing skills. Besides finding jobs at newspapers, music critics also work for magazines of the music genre.

Managing Musical Stars and Groups

A personal manager is a deal maker who oversees all aspects of an individual's or a group's musical career. This involves dealing with record companies, music publishers, booking agents, and merchandisers. It also means handling the promotion, publicity, touring, and concert logistics for the artist or group. Then there is the all-important job of managing the act's money. Finally, the personal manager must work constantly to develop the act's career and an audience for the act's music. For handling this wide variety of jobs, a manager makes from 10 to 50 percent of an act's gross; the typical manager takes from 15 to 20 percent. Working with a top artist or group can mean an income of more than $500,000 a year. Most personal managers usually handle one artist or group. There are also companies that handle several artists or groups and divide the responsibilities among a staff of professionals.

The one qualification successful personal managers have in common is an excellent knowledge of how the music industry works. Contacts within the industry are also extremely important in launching and maintaining an act's career. Furthermore, personal managers need to have a very good personal relationship with the individual artist or act. At one time almost all personal managers were located in New York or Los Angeles. While this is where most managers still are, many personal managers now live in the same area as their artists or groups.

Managing a Star

If you are familiar with the rock hit, "Hey Baby," then you know that Henry Lee Summer is the artist responsible for this song. The personal manager helping Henry Lee Summer go all the way to the top is James Bogard, who brings his considerable knowledge of the music industry to this task. During high school, James had his first introduction to the industry when he played in a professional band. After graduation from the Berklee College of Music in Boston, he learned even more about the music world as a performer with a soul group crisscrossing the country for more than five years. During this time, he acted as the eleven-member group's liaison with their manager, who taught him what was involved in being a manager through almost daily phone calls. He also had the opportunity to learn how to deal with nightclub owners, public relations people, and booking agents. After the group broke up, James became the manager of the rhythm section of the band and got the new band up and working, to the point of being offered a recording contract, but he could not keep the group together.

James then worked at a recording studio where he met artists who wanted to make their own records, including Henry Lee Summer. Henry Lee impressed James because he had talent, drive, and determination to go to the top. James left the studio and concentrated on Henry Lee—helping him with his records, booking his nightclub act, and working on recording projects. Then he became Henry Lee's personal manager, handling all aspects of this rising artist's career, including arranging for his client to be interviewed on popular television shows like *David Letterman* and *Arsenio Hall* and overseeing the companies Henry Lee owns. Top artists like Henry Lee usually have their own publishing, touring, and production companies and may have a record and even a movie company. Daily, James deals with all the people who want to work with with Henry Lee. James has an assistant who handles Henry Lee's personal financial planning and investments. Although James no longer performs, he enjoys working in the industry overseeing Henry Lee Summer's career.

Booking Entertainers for Special Events

Joe Deal is owner of Joe Deal Events, a company that does special event planning. His company handles every aspect of an event and can even come up with the theme or promotional idea for the function. Joe has a roster of talent that includes bands, musicians, and entertainers of all types. He matches what his clients are looking for with the talents from the roster.

Joe obtained a bachelor of science degree in a music business program. This is a relatively new degree program, which Joe liked because he could combine his love of music with business courses. To get this degree he needed not only four years of study at college but also had to complete two internships. He did one at a booking agency and the other at a music store.

Music Careers in Places of Worship

In churches and temples, music is an important part of religious worship, from the rhythm of African drums to the melodic voices of the Mormon Tabernacle Choir. For music lovers who have a knowledge of church music and a desire to work in a religious setting, there are jobs for music directors and choir directors. Qualifications for these jobs usually include a bachelor's or master's degree in music plus an ability to direct music performers. Full-time jobs in these positions are often limited to churches and temples having large congregations. About the only other jobs in this area are as assistants to music and choir directors.

Director of Music

Robert M. McBain, D.M.A., served for many years as director of music at Carmel Methodist Church. He has bachelor's and master's degrees in music as well as a doctoral degree. In addition, he has an instrumental conducting degree from the Mozarteum in Salzburg, Austria, and has done postdoctoral study with Donald Neuen at the Eastman School of Music in Rochester, New York.

As the son of a Baptist minister and an accomplished vocalist, Robert's first association with music was closely linked to his involvement in church music programs. Today, he has strong personal feelings about sharing his musical talent with his church. Throughout his years of study, Robert stayed involved with church music and also worked in the school system teaching choral music in secondary schools. Even though he was director of music, supervising all the music programs in a large church, he was also a general vocal music teacher in the public schools. Robert wants music lovers thinking of becoming church music directors to realize that it may be necessary to supplement their incomes, as he has done through the years with his teaching. The salary for directors of music varies greatly depending on the organization. For example, in some large churches in major cities music directors can earn as much as $100,000 annually. At the same time, many of these jobs are part-time with salaries starting as low as $4,000 a year.

As director of music at a church with twenty-six hundred members, Robert managed a staff that included a part-time children's choir director, a full-time organist, and a music associate. Besides the paid staff members, there were also a number of volunteers. Robert has been the music director of several other churches and has had staffs of fifty people reporting to him as well as being the only musician on staff. In many churches, the music director is also the choir director and organist.

In addition to his responsibilities as church music director and teacher, Robert was also director and conductor of the 150-member Carmel Symphonic Chorale and executive director of Music at Carmel, Inc., which puts on monthly concerts for the community. In the past, this versatile musician has been guest conductor at symphony orchestras in Oklahoma, Phoenix, Atlanta, and Indianapolis. He has also been the bass soloist for the Robert Schuller Hour of Power, sung with the Robert Shaw Choral, and recorded several albums.

Choir Director

Choir directors have the responsibility of directing the choir for church services. Directors also hold auditions for positions in the choir and work with section leaders, assistant conductors, and soloists. They must also select music, direct weekly rehearsals, plan special programs, and work closely with the other members of the music staff of the church.

Cantor

A cantor is a unique combination of minister, music director, teacher, and chief soloist in a synagogue. Janice Roger became a cantor because of her desire to express her love of Judaism through music. As a cantor, she is involved with music at all liturgical services for the public and in all areas of the life cycle—birth, marriage, and death.

Janice's background includes a bachelor's degree in music and a bachelor's degree in sacred music from a seminary, where she studied music for the synagogue as well as philosophy and religion. Immediately upon graduation from the seminary, Janice became a cantor for a large congregation. Her career satisfaction comes from watching young people grow and develop Jewish identities. She believes a cantor most visibly helps members of congregations by elevating their spiritual lives through music.

The requirements for becoming a cantor are not consistent throughout the Reform movement. It may or may not be necessary to have attended a seminary. The employment outlook for cantors is good because there are many more positions than there are people to fill them.

More Job Information for Music Lovers

The available possibilities of a job associated with music are much greater than most people imagine. For example, whenever music lovers hear music, they should ask themselves where the music came from and who wrote, sold, marketed, or packaged the music. Then they should investigate possible jobs in such areas as background music, telephone music, the military, and piano tuning. Music lovers can also learn more about job opportunities by reading books and brochures like the following ones that detail the duties, salary ranges, and job qualifications for numerous positions associated with music.

For More Information

Brochures

American Symphony Orchestra League. 1156 15th Street NW, Suite 800, Washington, DC 20005. Information about careers in orchestra management.

Careers in Music. Music Educators National Conference. 1806 Robert Fulton Drive, Reston, VA 20191-4348.

National Association for Music Therapy, Inc. 8455 Colesville Road, Suite 1000, Silver Spring, MD 20910. Information about careers in music therapy.

Books

Bjorneberg, Paul, compiler. *Exploring Careers in Music.* Reston, VA: Music Educators National Conference, 1990.

Field, Shelly. *Career Opportunities in the Music Industry.* New York: Facts on File, 1995.

Gerardi, Robert. *Opportunities in Music Careers.* Lincolnwood, IL: VGM Career Horizons, 1997.

Johnson, Jeff. *Careers for Music Lovers & Other Tuneful Types.* Lincolnwood, IL: VGM Career Horizons, 1997.

CHAPTER FOUR

Careers for Dance Lovers

Enjoying Dance from Ballet to Swing

"Will you, won't you, will you, won't you join the dance?"
LEWIS CARROLL, *Alice's Adventures in Wonderland*

D ancing is fun for children and adults. It is the language of the body that lets us show our feelings and thoughts through movement. Children can't stay still when they hear the beat of music nor can many adults who dance for the pure joy of moving their bodies to music. Dancing has played a major role in culture through the ages. Primitive people drew pictures on cave walls in Spain depicting people dancing more than fifty thousand years ago. Many peoples have folk dances that have been passed down from generation to generation and are still being performed, like the Highland fling of Scotland, the German polka, and American folk dances. Dance is considered the mother of other arts. The first music was created as a rhythm for early dances. Artists and sculptors through the ages have been inspired to create masterpieces showing the grace of dancers. And it is believed that the drama of most countries originated in their dances. Today, more than ever before, people are viewing professional performances of dance and participating in dance activities from lessons to social dancing to dance exercise classes.

Because dance is currently so popular, there are good opportunities to find a career associated with dancing. Dance lovers do not need to be performers to find careers involved with dancing; however, a knowledge of dance is required for certain jobs.

Teachers are needed at all levels, from preschool dance classes to classes for professional dancers. Choreographers are needed to design the movements that go with the music in different dances. Dance performances are enhanced by the individuals who have created the costumes, scenery, and lighting. Dance therapists work in hospitals, clinics, and other rehabilitation centers to help people regain movement. Movement analysts help people eliminate poor movement habits and get rid of muscle tension by teaching them neuromuscular reeducation techniques. Dance historians, critics, and writers are needed at libraries, dance companies, and newspapers and magazines to communicate their knowledge of dance to the public. There are even dance medicine assistants—trainers, nurses, and doctors who use their knowledge of anatomy and understanding of body movements as they relate to dance to help restore people to improved health. Without question, there are countless jobs for dance lovers. At the same time, you must realize that few of them are nine-to-five jobs, since so many are associated with performances.

Choreographers

Choreographers create new dances and dance productions, modify or adapt existing dances, and integrate dance sections into shows. They are to dancers what the composer is to music. The choreographer is the key person in a dance company. It is the choreographer's job to know what the human body can do and to use that knowledge to teach the dancers how to move their bodies in the performance of a dance. The choreographer also works with the dance company's costume designer and lighting director to produce an integrated performance.

Most choreographers are self-taught. They learn to choreograph from their own personal dance experiences or by watching other choreographers work. Choreographers draw upon their own experiences to come up with ideas for dances. At times, the music provides the idea; at other times, the movement comes first and the music is added later. Choreographers must possess more than a knowledge of dance and music. They need to understand lighting, stage dimensions, and cameras. Their jobs will vary from company to company. However, choreographers are usually expected to teach the company dance class, choreograph pieces for the company, rehearse the dancers, choose the dance repertoire, and select guest choreographers to work with the company.

Job Opportunities

As dancing flourishes, so does the need for choreographers in dance companies; opera companies; movie, television, and video productions; theaters; and nightclub shows. New avenues are opening up for choreographers. For example, in the area of ice dancing they are helping skaters perform more exquisite patterns on the ice and in the air. Roller skating is another area in which choreographers are able to help coordinate their movements to the music. With innovations such as electronic sounds and music videos, choreography is becoming an even more challenging career for talented and creative individuals.

Salaries

The earnings of choreographers with dance companies are specified by the Society of Stage Directors and Choreographers. Choreographers of Broadway shows receive a weekly fee, an advance, and a minimum royalty. Fees for off-Broadway productions, nonprofit productions, and stock productions vary depending upon such things as size of theater and length of engagement. Earnings from fees and performance royalties range from about $1,000 a week in small professional theaters to more than $30,000 for an eight- to ten-week rehearsal period for a Broadway production. In high-budget films, choreographers make $3,400 for a five-day week; in television, $8,000 to $12,500 for up to fourteen workdays.

Notators and Reconstructors

Ballet companies throughout the world often want to reproduce the work of a great choreographer even though the choreographer may be either dead or simply unable to come and train their dancers. Since the 1920s, it has been possible to record every movement of a ballet because a system of dance notation was developed. This system, known as labanotation, uses special symbols to record every movement of a ballet. Special training is necessary to learn this symbol system. Many universities offer training in labanotation.

Notators used to produce the score of a dance with pencil and a ruler. Then an autographer would hand copy the score in ink or type it. With the advent of the computer, notators are now able to use a program to record each step, and the need for autographers is rapidly disappearing. Individuals who can read a completed score and teach it to dancers are called reconstructors. Most reconstructors are college professors who do the work of restaging dances as freelancers. There is a very limited demand for the specialized skills of notators and reconstructors.

Dance Kaleidoscope—a Contemporary Dance Company

When dance lovers think of working for a dance company, they may immediately think of well-known companies such as New York City Ballet, American Ballet Theater, the Joffrey Ballet, San Francisco Ballet, or Alvin Ailey American Dance Theater. While these organizations have many jobs for dance lovers, a great number can also be found with smaller companies located in almost every region of the United States. To find where some of these dance companies are located, job seekers should consult *Stern's Performing Arts Directory* at a public library.

Dance lovers in Indiana have found satisfying jobs with Dance Kaleidoscope, a contemporary dance company started in 1972. It is the only professional contemporary dance company in Indiana. The company's mission is to bring the finest in choreography from around the world to its audiences. The eight-member company presents four subscriptions series a year. When members are not on stage, they perform for schoolchildren. The company also performs nationwide on tour. During the summer, Dance Kaleidoscope is in residence at the Ashland, Oregon, Shakespeare Festival, where they perform six times a week before productions. Because this company is small, staff members may do several jobs that would be handled by different individuals at a larger company.

Artistic Director

David Hochoy is the artistic director of Dance Kaleidoscope and is therefore responsible for the way the company looks during a performance. He has to make sure that everything happens as scheduled and that all the elements run together smoothly to make the correct technical and artistic presentation. David also teaches the company's daily dance class, choreographs dances for the company, rehearses the dancers, chooses the company's repertoire, selects guest choreographers, and works with the lighting designer, production manager, technical director, and costume designer.

Because the company is small, David must do many other jobs. One of the most important is going out into the community to tell people about Dance Kaleidoscope. David envisioned what this company would be like and what it was going to become. He publicizes this vision with every form of media so that the vision will become a reality. David also serves as a figurehead for the company for fund-raising activities.

Career Path

During his high school years, David became deeply involved with the arts as he studied piano, participated in the school choir, drew and painted, was a member of theater groups, participated in some theatrical productions, and entered public speaking contests. In college, he obtained a master's degree in theater but then decided against getting a doctorate because he preferred being a performer to being a member of the academic community. Knowing that he wanted to be a dancer, David went to New York City, dance center of the United States with the greatest number of companies. For several years, his life was a combination of working as a waiter at night and taking dance classes during the day. Then he took different jobs with small dance companies in New York and worked in Toronto for a year before joining the Martha Graham Dance Theater, where he stayed for ten years. He began with the company as an ordinary dancer, became a soloist and then a rehearsal director. As a rehearsal director, David was no longer dancing; instead, he was directing the other dancers through their rehearsals. At the same time, he was also doing his own choreography and making his own dances. He became more interested in doing these things and decided to leave the company to go to Texas Christian University. For two years, as an assistant professor, David taught modern dance techniques, composition, and dance repertoire, while choreographing student productions, counseling the students, and supervising student productions.

A Challenging Job

Today, David finds his job at Dance Kaleidoscope to be challenging and compares it to overcoming the obstacles in climbing Mt. Everest and just as rewarding. This is the only job that David is interested in doing, even if he is on call twenty-four hours a day. He usually works an eight- to twelve-hour day; however, the closer it gets to a performance, the hours increase and it is not uncommon for him to put in sixteen-hour days. In his free time, David loves to watch other dance companies. He listens to music all the time because he is always trying to find new music to use in choreographing a new number for the dance company.

Director of Operations

It's the task of the director of operations at Dance Kaleidoscope to hold things together on the business side. According to the company job description for this position, Janice Virgin, who is the director of operations, is expected to oversee all aspects of the day-to-day management of the administrative office, including budget, communication between board and staff, meetings pertaining to office operations, systems maintenance, and correspondence and reports as needed. Additionally, this position requires her to coordinate staff/volunteer support for the lobby and the Dance Kaleidoscope boutique at concerts. With such a broad job description, Janice finds herself doing a variety of tasks each day. Because she typically arrives first each morning, her day begins as she turns on the equipment to get the office ready. During the course of the day, she may handle such tasks as proofing programs, making badges, hiring new employees, acting as the secretary at board meetings, monitoring supplies, handling complimentary ticket requests, making deposits, soliciting advertising for the season program, maintaining records regarding subscriptions and single ticket sales, getting mailings out, and generally seeing that the Dance Kaleidoscope office is running smoothly. On performance days, her job extends to supervising the ushers and the operation of the boutique booth in the lobby.

Career Path

Throughout her life, Janice has been an avid culture lover. She learned to appreciate classical music from her father, a concert pianist who filled their home with music. And she was only five when her love of dance emerged and she began to take ballet lessons, which she continued for thirteen years. In college, Janice concentrated on training in medicine as her family wished her to have a more solid career than they believed she could have in the arts. For a number of years after college, she worked in medicine and then as a special education and reading teacher. When one of her children, a talented dancer, began to tour with a dance company, Janice returned to the arts. Not only did she act as a chaperone for her daughter, she also danced profession-ally with the company in bit parts. Then she became a full-time administrative assistant for the ballet company and was the assis-tant marketing and development/box office manager when she left the company for her current position with Dance Kaleido-scope. Janice especially likes her job as director of operations because she believes that she is part of a team in which each member—whether on the artistic or business side—appreciates everyone's contribution to the success of the company.

Director of Touring and Education

In his job with Dance Kaleidoscope, Tim Hubbard wears two hats as is typical in smaller dance companies. Tim is both the director of touring and of education, a new position at Dance Kaleidoscope. As director of touring, he is responsible for book-ing dance company performances throughout the United States. And in the next few years, he sees the possibility of international bookings. In order to secure bookings, Tim has to build rela-tionships with presenters and sponsors. Part of getting the atten-tion of potential bookers involves attending four or five booking conferences each year where he sets up a booth with information about Dance Kaleidoscope. Being director of touring involves far more, however, than booking events. Tim is in charge of tour and travel arrangements and tour contracts. He also has to make sure that each tour site meets the technical requirements for a show and that press marketing kits are available. In this job, he is always looking ahead.

Dance Kaleidoscope evolved from the Young Audiences of Indiana program, which links the arts to schoolchildren, and still has a partnership with this organization. During the year, the company presents many in-school programs to acquaint children with dance. Also, the company is active in bringing students to shows and giving them an in-depth look at the performers. As director of education, Tim is in charge of getting schools involved in the arts through activities of Dance Kaleidoscope. Part of his job lies in finding sponsorships so more programs can be offered. He truly likes his work as director of education, as the company is so focused on making children aware of the arts.

Career Path

The arts have always played a role in Tim's life. Although he was older when he knew that he wanted to become a dancer, Tim was able to have a thirteen-year career as a performer. During that time, he was a founding member of a small ballet company in which he always had to be ready to handle whatever came up. Besides teaching dance, he choreographed for the company and worked as a lighting designer and as a technical director. He also oversaw all the touring and production work. Dance Kaleidoscope offered him his current position with the mission of taking the education and touring activities of the group to a different level.

Costume Designer

Barry Doss was a resident freelance costume designer for Dance Kaleidoscope for several years until he left for New York City to work on Broadway musicals and for costuming firms. In the dance company, he worked with David Hochoy, the artistic director, to create the appropriate costume designs for each performance. Because he worked with dancers, Barry had to make sure that the costumes would not only have artistic value but first and foremost be functional for the dancers. Costumes are different for different types of dancing, and the designer must know exactly what is needed. For example, because in ballet there is only limited movement of the upper torso, many costumes designed for the ballerina even have metal stays, while costumes for modern dance need to be designed so that the torso is free to move.

The Steps in Designing Costumes

As a costume designer, Barry watches the choreographer work with the dancers to get a design concept. The first step is to draw sketches to turn what the director wants into two-dimensional images that will give Barry a reference point from which he can work. The reference point gives lines and colors and actual shapes. In the artistic world, such a drawing is called a rendering.

After the costume designer and the choreographer come to an agreement on a rendering, the fabric needs to be selected. Samples are gathered and brought back to the director for approval. Once the fabric selection has been made, it must be cut or draped. Muslin is used to drape and cut the pattern out directly on the form. When the drafts method is used, a pattern is cut and then the pattern is used to cut out the material. At Dance Kaleidoscope Barry did all of this himself. In a larger company, he would have assistants. After the garment has been constructed, it is then fitted on the dancer so that the costume designer can check that it allows freedom of movement. Alterations can be made easily at this point before the final sewing. Then the costume is ready for the final sewing, followed by the finishing work. Finishing work means adding all the trim, glitter, rhinestones, buttons, snaps, and hooks and eyes that are needed for the costume. With the finishing work complete, the costume is ready for the dancer to come in for a final fitting.

On performance night at Dance Kaleidoscope, Barry could be found backstage if he was needed. However, he preferred to sit out front enjoying the show and seeing how all the hours of hard work had paid off. Costumes look different in the costume studio than when they are on the dancers under the stage lights, so Barry has to make sure that when the curtain goes up on a performance, everything is just as he and the director planned it.

Career Path

Barry holds a bachelor of arts in theater, with a double emphasis in acting performance and costume design and a minor in interior and fashion design. He attended college on an acting scholarship in theater and selected Texas Christian University in Fort Worth, Texas, the first university in the country to have a department for ballet and modern dance. Before this department was created, dancers had to study in a conservatory rather than on a university campus. In college, Barry became actively involved in ballet and costuming when he worked on the ballet *Scheherezade*. He was the assistant designer for the production, which in this case meant doing most of the accessory work, such as headpieces.

At the university, he met David Hochoy and was so impressed with his choreography in *Starry Night*, a production based on the van Gogh painting with Philip Glass music, that he offered to work for David anytime he needed a costume designer. Barry got the chance to work with him at the school on *Young Apollo*, a production set to Nat King Cole's music. Barry had to design four costumes for the production—costumes for a young man and three muses. Since *Young Apollo* is a mythical piece with a modern twist, the muses had to look like goddesses—but not in the traditional sense. To achieve this difficult assignment, Barry used lots of colors.

In his free time, this culture lover enjoys going to the theater, history and art museums, and large spectacular musical shows like *Les Misérables*. He also enjoys shopping for antiques, going to arts and crafts shows, and attending dance performances. From all these visual experiences, he is able to gather ideas and inspirations for his own work. Barry feels that being a costume designer requires versatility. During your schooling you study costume designing for dance, theater, films, television, and commercials before choosing an area in which to specialize.

More Jobs with Dance Companies

At one time, dance lovers would have had trouble finding jobs with dance companies outside of New York City and major cities such as Chicago and San Francisco. Now there are hundreds of small companies. Unfortunately, these companies do not have large staffs of administrators. When they first start, many just have a director, but as they win acclaim they add general managers; marketing, development, and operations staff; accountants; and other administrative support. Some companies don't hire their own staffs but obtain the management help they need from a company that offers support services to several dance or other performing arts companies. Dance lovers should also consider jobs with these firms.

Teaching Dance—the Training of Dance Lovers

Children just naturally dance; they can hardly keep their bodies still. Throughout their lives, most people continue loving to dance. Millions of dollars are spent every year for dance lessons for preschoolers learning to tap and do ballet, for high school students learning social dancing, and for adults brushing up on their ballroom dance steps or simply exercising through dance. Professional ballet dancers even take lessons or daily practice classes to stay in top physical condition. Teachers are needed to train all these eager dancers in a variety of settings, such as day care centers, nursing homes, state hospitals, public schools, dance schools, colleges, studios, conservatories, and special education programs. Your dream of teaching dance can even extend to owning your own dance studio. Job opportunities appear to be best for dance lovers seeking employment as dance teachers in private studios and schools.

Teaching dance gives dance lovers an opportunity not only to be closely involved with dance but to actually dance on the job. Do you think that you possess the necessary special skills and knowledge to be a dance teacher? Ask yourself the following questions:

1. Do you have an anatomical understanding of how the body works?

2. Do you have the ability to relate to people of different ages?

3. Do you enjoy music?

4. Do you have the ability to choreograph dances for other people?

5. Do you have the patience to teach the same step over and over?

6. Do you have the organizational skills needed to break a dance down into parts and then reteach each part until the whole dance has been mastered?

7. Do you have the skills necessary to keep discipline in a class?

8. Do you possess a sense of rhythm?

9. Are you able to express ideas, moods, and emotions through dance movements?

10. Are you self-confident?

11. Are you creative?

12. Are you able to work under pressure at times?

13. Do you have ambition?

14. Do you have talent?

15. Are you willing to spend long hours in training and practice?

16. Do you have good physical endurance?

17. Do you have leadership ability?

18. Do you have a sincere interest and love of dancing?

Dance lovers truly qualified to become dance teachers will answer "Yes" to almost every one of the above questions. To actually teach dance, the training and educational background needed will depend on the type of dance you wish to teach and where you want to teach. Many private dance teachers have trained since early childhood, and their own personal background acts as the foundation of their teaching. Most of these dancers will continue their own lessons and practice sessions even after they have started to teach dance. Dance lovers who want to teach in a public school, however, will need to have bachelor's degrees and credentials just like other teachers in the educational system.

Earnings

The average salaries of teachers in private practice vary widely, depending on the number of hours they work and the places of employment. Salaries range between $10,000 and more than $30,000 a year. Dance teachers in public schools and colleges earn the same salaries as other teachers.

A Dance Teacher with His Own Studio

Russell Clark is the regional dance director for the Arthur Murray International Dance Organization, which has a network of 250 franchised dance studios in the United States. His duties are twofold, as he has to train both dance instructors and dance students. Russell is also a judicator for the world professional dance teachers' organization. In this capacity, he judges dance competitions in the Midwest region comprising thirteen states, as well as international competitions.

Russell began his dance career immediately after completing high school. He took a four-week training program at the franchised studio where he was going to work. This just whetted his appetite for dance, so he started taking lessons in different areas, including tap, ballet, and jazz. Since his first lessons, he has studied and practiced every day for at least two hours. With his lessons completed, Russell began teaching in Chicago and worked with new students, giving them their first twenty lessons in ballroom dancing. He worked his way up the dance studio career ladder to become a supervisor. At this level, Russell trained all new students and was even training teachers. In this business, Russell points out, teachers need to be trained in inter-personal skills as well as in technical teaching skills, for they must help their students relax and overcome nervousness. It is also important for teachers to be able to explain in a clear way what the students need to do to accomplish their goals.

Teaching dance in a studio is definitely not a nine-to-five job. Most teachers work a sixty-hour week and spend at least two to three hours additionally every day working on their own danc-ing. Owning a dance studio franchise as Russell now does means even more work and responsibilities; he must not only attract new students, but also needs to keep them coming back. At the present time, he is planning to add a baby-sitting area, which should appeal to young couples because it will let them bring their children to the studio. When you own a dance franchise, you are running a small business. You will probably need to have a lawyer and a bookkeeper. You will be keeping records, collect-ing fees, paying taxes, keeping track of renewal dates, and fol-lowing local, state, and federal business and tax laws. In addition, to keep your business going you will need to have a long-range development plan.

Russell has been successful with his dance studio franchise. He believes that interest in dancing is growing and that people who are willing to devote enormous amounts of time and effort can have successful franchise operations. He now has two loca-tions and six to ten employees at each location.

There is no question that Russell is a confirmed dance lover. Besides working in the field, for recreation he and his wife go out dancing at least twice a week and still perform together. Furthermore, he still enjoys dancing just as much as when he started after completing high school and was new to the dance business.

A Teacher of Ballroom, Exercise Dancing, and Ballet

Johanna Bruyn is owner of Johanna's World of Dance Incorporated. She was born in Indonesia and lived in the Netherlands before coming to the United States. As a child, she danced all the time. She had to abandon hopes for a dance career because of limited finances when her family moved to this country. Nevertheless, she never forgot her love of dance and always remembered the thrill she had turning and twirling as a young ballerina. Dance with all its joys came back into her life when she was twenty-seven and started going to discos. For three years, she drove to Chicago every weekend and trained with Charles and Rosemary Mattison. The Mattisons had impressive credentials as teachers, having won the prestigious Harvest Moon Ball dance contest. They used the prize money to open a studio to train others. Many of their students have also gone on to win the Harvest Moon Ball contest.

Johanna started teaching dance at the Free University in Indianapolis in 1976 with Jim Skolburg. Their classes always had from sixty to eighty people at each session. The Free University was just getting started at this time, and the money which was made from the dance classes helped the university to take off and become a viable school in the community. Johanna also started taking lessons from her current mentors, Dale Willman and Lee Harris. According to Johanna, lessons are always essential for dance teachers to keep their skills sharp and to pass on the latest steps to their students.

For almost six years Johanna operated her own studio; now she offers dance programs at clubs and community centers and as part of adult/community education programs. She enjoys the flexibility of doing dance at different places. Johanna is such a successful teacher that she and her students have even danced the Viennese waltz in performance with the Indianapolis Symphony Orchestra. She also uses her background to teach a form of exercise workout she invented that uses jazz. Johanna likes a more stylized form of exercise than the usual aerobics. In her workout, there is more choreography and lots of stretches and isometrics. It is a low-impact form of exercise.

Johanna does not limit her teaching to her jazz workout or ballroom dancing. After she learned the art of teaching ballet from Virginia Holte, Johanna began teaching ballet; she now teaches more than one hundred little ballerinas. Her preschool classes have children from two and a half to five years old. Most ballet schools will not work with children this young. She gets all of her business from the word-of-mouth advertising of her satisfied students and a small ad in the yellow pages.

A Teacher of Social Dancing and Etiquette

Rebecca Kreuger Malenkos majored in English in college and became a high school English teacher, but her true love is dancing, which has always been a part of her life. She started taking dance lessons at the age of four and studied ballet, tap, jazz, and ballroom dancing for more than thirteen years. In high school, she not only danced but was also in the choir and musical productions. By the time Rebecca was in tenth grade, she had become a student assistant at the ballroom dancing school for young people where she had taken lessons in social dancing and etiquette since she was in sixth grade. She gained even more teaching experience in college through teaching ballroom dancing at Wake Forest University and at a neighboring women's college. Her six-week courses for college students were a way for the students to not only learn to dance but also to meet each other in a social situation. After college, Rebecca operated her own school in Texas called Rebecca's Cotillion, where she taught dance etiquette and such basic ballroom dances as the fox trot, waltz, swing, and tango. After moving to Indianapolis, she reopened Rebecca's Cotillion. There is more than teaching dance to operating her school. Students have to receive written invitations, publicity must be done to advertise the school, and she has to solve the logistical problem of having an equal number of boys and girls for each class.

A College Professor of Dance

Stephan Laurent is the chair of the department of dance at Butler University and also an associate professor at the university. Like so many dance teachers, Stephan was a professional dancer with a long performance career before he started to teach. He didn't start studying dance until almost twenty, which is rather late for a professional dancer to begin.

Stephan interrupted his performance career to study at Southern Methodist University, where he received both his bachelor's and master's degrees. He became an associate professor of dance at the University of Wisconsin-Milwaukee, leaving there to become the artistic director of the Des Moines Ballet, now known as Ballet Iowa. Stephan then chose to move to Butler University, where 45 percent of the school's dance graduates go on to have a professional performing career—one of the highest number of graduates in the country to go into professional careers. In his present job, Stephan supervises the dance faculty, establishes the curriculum, and choreographs productions. Because the Butler Ballet Company is run like a professional company and puts on five or six shows a year, there is considerable choreographing for all the faculty members to do. Students also get a chance to choreograph, though the dance company is run by the faculty. Stephan explains that jobs like his at the university level require incredible dedication, energy, and physical, mental, and emotional endurance. They also allow dance lovers to be closely involved with several aspects of dancing.

Organizations for Dance Teachers

Dance lovers who are considering a career in the teaching of dance should contact dance associations for solid career information. Prospective dance teachers should also read the publications of these associations to keep abreast of what is happening in dance. And they should consider attending association conventions to meet dance teachers and watch demonstrations of the latest dance techniques.

The following dance organizations can provide helpful information to dance teachers.

American Dance Teachers Association; Vienna, Virginia

American Society of Russian Style Ballet; Boston, Massachusetts

Associated Dance Teachers of New Jersey; Chatham, New Jersey

British Dance Teachers Association; Montana, California

Canadian Dance Teachers Association; Vancouver, British Columbia

Ceccheti Council of America; Detroit, Michigan

Chicago National Association of Dance Masters; Chicago, Illinois

Dance Educators of America; Caldwell, New Jersey

Dance Masters of America, Inc.; Orlando, Florida

Golden State Dance Teachers Association; Downey, California

Imperial Society of Teachers of Dancing (U.S. Ballroom Branch); Nashua, New Hampshire

International Dance Seminars, Inc.; Long Beach, New York

Arthur Murray, Inc.; Coral Gables, Florida

National Association of Dance & Affiliated Artists, Inc.; Millbrae, California

National Council of Dance Teachers Organizations; Richmond Hill, New York

New York Society of Teachers of Dancing; Bellmore, New York

Professional Dance Teachers Association, Inc.; Waldwick, New Jersey

Southern Association of Dance Masters, Inc.; Lonoke, Arizona

Southern Oregon Dance Association, Inc.; Oakland, Oregon

Texas Teachers of Dancing; Lubbock, Texas

United States Dance Teachers Association; Los Angeles, California

Dance/Movement Therapy—Better Health Through Dancing

Dance/movement therapists use movement to improve the physical and emotional health of the people with whom they are working. The American Dance Therapy Association defines dance/movement therapy as the psychotherapeutic use of movement as a process that furthers the emotional and physical integration of the individual.

To become a dance/movement therapist, dance lovers need to complete both an undergraduate program with emphasis in psychology and training in a variety of dance forms, followed by professional training at the graduate level and an internship. You also need to be able to perform, choreograph, and teach dance.

Dance/ movement therapists need to have a strong desire to work with others and the patience, dedication, and stamina to get the job done.

The moving body is the medium of the dance/movement therapist's work. The therapist focuses on the communicative, expressive, and adaptive aspects of nonverbal behavior, using these to help clients effect changes in thinking, feelings, physical functioning, and behavior. The method consists of structuring and guiding bodily experience toward an expression of wholeness and self-awareness. This involves:

- identification and release of psycho-emotional-physical blocks in the body, thereby increasing range of motion

- increasing the dynamic range of the body's movement options or patterns

- providing a clear and safe context for the client to connect present bodily experience with past and present emotional traumas and/or issues

- facilitating a creative, imaginative, exploratory atmosphere where clients are able to discover and establish new patterns for interacting with others

Most dance/movement therapists work in psychiatric hospitals and community health centers. Jobs are also available in hospitals, special schools, rehabilitation centers, developmental centers, correctional facilities, and nursing homes. Dance/movement therapy is a relatively new career. At the present time, these therapists do not need a state license to practice. The American Dance Therapy Association distinguishes between therapists who are prepared to work within a team or under supervision and those who can work independently. Therapists with the title Dance Therapist Registered (DTR) have a master's degree and are fully qualified to work in a professional treatment system. Therapists with the title Academy of Dance Therapists

Registered (ADTR) have met additional requirements and are fully qualified to teach, provide supervision, and engage in private practice.

Dance/movement therapists work with a variety of populations, including the emotionally disturbed or physically disabled; with children, adolescents, and older people; in group and individual sessions. They can also provide valuable information to a treatment team on a client's status and behavioral patterns, make assessments, and propose movement-based interventions. Dance/movement therapy encourages the client to take an active role in her or his own process of gaining or regaining health and an optimal level of functioning.

A Dance/Movement Therapist

James Lobley, DTR, is a dance/movement therapist. He does both individual and group movement therapy in working with children from the ages of three to twelve. James also does family therapy through dance. The types of children with whom he works include special needs children, developmentally delayed children, children with social and emotional difficulties, and children who have been sexually abused. As a dance/movement therapist, he teaches social skills and helps children learn the proper outlet for their feelings. Dance/movement therapy uses a holistic approach in the way it perceives movement as an integral part of the whole human being. Through physical movements, dance/movement therapists are able to change people on a deeper psychological level; they can also affect how clients perceive themselves. James has used fairy tales and creative movement to address the developmental, personal, and interpersonal issues of children.

In college, James majored in French and semiotics at Brown University. After graduation, he danced for two years, while serving as an apprentice in woodworking. After a short while, he decided that he would rather work with people than inanimate objects, so he entered a two-year dance/movement therapy program at New York University. Few colleges in the United States have master's programs in dance/movement therapy. Becoming a registered dance/movement therapist is a long process involving a master's degree plus a seven hundred-hour internship. James did his internship at a private school for language-impaired children on Long Island. Returning to Indianapolis, at a local hospital he led movement recreational activities and gender and psychotherapy groups. He also has assisted in development of treatment plans, offered individual counseling, and served as family liaison at a hospital.

Movement Analyst Specialist

As an assistant professor at Butler University, Idrienne Sobel-Steiman taught ballet dance to majors as well as dance therapists, fitness instructors, and other college students interested in understanding and changing movement of the body. Idrienne is a certified movement analyst. Most jobs for movement analysts are found in the college setting. Idrienne taught classes in body alignment, Laban Movement Analysis, and improvisation. In teaching these classes, she drew upon her background in three movement reeducation methods to teach the students techniques for changing poor or inefficient movement habits. She also used these techniques to teach them how to prevent injuries and strengthen their bodies. Idrienne worked mostly with ballet students. In the past twenty years, the process of teaching dance has become more anatomically and scientifically based as dancers want to learn more about movement. This has resulted in a demand for college teachers, like Idrienne, who can teach the science of dance.

Idrienne's educational background includes bachelor's and master's degrees in dance. She also has taken ballet lessons since she was eight, studying at such prestigious schools of dance as Juilliard and Joffrey and spending a summer at *Le Centre de Danse International* in Cannes, France. In pursuing her original career choice of becoming a dancer, she worked with wonderful teachers like Andre Eglevskey from Russia, Melissa Hayden at Skidmore College, and her mentor, Marty Morginsky, who took her under his wing and helped and inspired her to develop the talent she had.

Career Path

Idrienne's career path includes jobs both in the dance and business worlds. After completing her bachelor's degree, Idrienne needed to find a job and got one in arts administration at the Joffrey Ballet. This job was a full-time, forty-hour-a-week job, so she danced every evening in classes taught by Finis Jhung and David Howard. Idrienne's next career move was to decide she really wanted to teach and not dance in a company. To make sure this decision was right for her, she tried the business world, working on Wall Street in commodities and then at what she calls a great job with *Vogue* magazine, which didn't satisfy her because her heart remained with dancing.

So after working in many different fields, she went to graduate school to get her master's in dance. During this time, she was teaching dance and dance workshops and working for physical therapists using her knowledge of therapeutic exercise, as well as seeing private patients. At this point in her life, she was juggling a variety of jobs including performing with the Joffrey company when it came to California, choreographing, and even performing as a movie extra. She also began to study with body therapists in the Los Angeles area and started to understand body therapies and the relationship of the mind and the body and how the mind affects movement. With this knowledge of dance and body movement, Idrienne knew she wanted to help people become more aware of themselves through movement, help them get rid of pain through movement, and enable them to function better in their lives whether they were dancers or secretaries or accountants. If Idrienne had to describe her career in the dance world, she would explain how she went from being a dancer who always wanted to perform to becoming an educator in a new field of dance.

More Information About Dance Careers

Dance is the most fundamental of the arts, as it gives people the opportunity to directly express themselves through their bodies. Not only is dance a powerful form of expression, it is a powerful medium for therapy. The job outlook is good for dancers and culture lovers looking for jobs with regional companies or dance groups connected with colleges. With the general interest in dance increasing, the opportunities for employment in other areas aligned with dance have also increased, so dance lovers may be able to find a career niche closely associated with some aspect of dance.

You will be able to obtain additional information about colleges and universities offering degrees in dance by contacting one of the following organizations:

National Dance Association, a Division of the American Alliance for Health, Physical Education, Recreation, and Dance, 1900 Association Drive, Reston, VA 20191-1599

The American Guild of Musical Artists, 1727 Broadway, New York, NY 10019

American Dance Therapy Association, Suite 108, 2000 Century Plaza, Columbia, MD 21044

In addition, *Dance Magazine* publishes a College Guide Directory to dance in North American colleges and universities, which is available in some libraries or by contacting *Dance Magazine*, 33 West Sixtieth Street, New York, NY 10023.

To be more knowledgeable about the career opportunities that exist in dance, dance lovers should investigate such dance-oriented publications as *Dance Magazine*, *Dance Teacher Now*, *Dance and the Arts*, and *Ballet Review*.

American Dance Guild

One dance organization that can provide valuable information to all who have or want to have careers in some aspect of dance is the American Dance Guild (ADG). The guild was founded in 1956 by a group of New York dance professionals seeking services and information in the pursuit of excellence within the field. The guild has become a multiservice organization providing a forum for the exchange of ideas and methods through its publications, conferences, and seminars. The ADG provides representation to national arts and education policy groups and an informed voice on behalf of dance to government agencies, corporations, and the public at large. This organization works to achieve Isadora Duncan's vision, "I see America dancing!"

The American Dance Guild can help dance lovers by providing:

- a Web site (http://www.americandanceguild.org) that has a variety of bibliographies on dance resource books

- a journal of American dance

- information about the Guild's major national conference which brings prominent professionals in dance together with ADG members and the public to share ideas

- a forum for the exchange of ideas through conferences, publications, the Dance Resource Center, and special interest groups

- job information through the Web site

- career guidance for students and professionals in transition on the Web site

- a student scholarship program

- a speakers bureau on the Web site

- mailing lists to dance enthusiasts

In addition, the ADG has career information for the following dance careers:

Administration/Management	Historian
Choreography	Notator
College/University	Performer
Community Studios/Centers	Researcher
Critic/Writer	Studio
Elementary/High School	Therapist

If you want information from the ADG, send a self-addressed, stamped business-sized envelope to the American Dance Guild, P.O. Box 2006, Lenox Hill Station, New York, NY 10021.

CHAPTER FIVE

Careers for Theater Lovers
Enjoying the World Behind the Stage

"As in a theatre, the eyes of men,
After a well-grac'd actor leaves the stage,
Are idly bent on him that enters next..." SHAKESPEARE, *Richard III*

A theatrical performance is always an exciting event whether it is on Broadway or in a small community theater. The attention of the audience is focused closely on the actors as the plot of a comedy, drama, or musical unfolds. At the end of the performance, the audience claps approval of what they have seen. It is not, however, just the work of the actors that they are applauding.

Theater is a very complex art that requires many specialists to create a production. In the most sophisticated Broadway presentations, producers, directors, set designers, costume designers, lighting designers, sound designers, stagehands, and business staff are all needed to create a play. In musical productions, choreographers, conductors, and orchestras are also required. In fact, all theatrical productions have to have many people behind the stage. In small companies, many handle more than one job or are volunteers gaining valuable career experience.

Where Theater Lovers Find Jobs

Not just in large cities but throughout the United States, groups are producing plays. Wherever plays are produced, there are jobs or opportunities to gain experience as unpaid volunteers. When theater lovers think of jobs in the theater, they may automatically think of jobs on Broadway, since it has achieved so much fame. There are, however, many other commercial (for profit) theaters besides Broadway, although the latter generally require the largest staff. Off-Broadway theaters have smaller productions in smaller theaters and less staff than Broadway productions. Community theaters usually depend on volunteers, except for a paid director for a production. Other opportunities for jobs in commercial theater exist in stock and dinner theaters, although stock productions usually only operate on a seasonal basis. Successful Broadway productions frequently spawn national touring companies that play in major cities like Chicago, Washington, and Los Angeles. Then smaller companies are formed to tour less populous areas. In addition, some companies mount theatrical productions for industrial shows.

More people are employed in nonprofit theater than commercial theater. The greatest number of jobs is found in the theaters that are members of the League of Resident Theaters (LORT), a group of equity theaters including the American Conservatory Theater (ACT) in San Francisco, the Arena Stage in Washington, and the Actor's Theatre in Louisville, Kentucky. Other theaters in the nonprofit sector include off-off-Broadway theaters, theaters on college campuses, and children's companies. Employment in off-off-Broadway theaters is usually for one play, and the staff receive very low wages. Some college theaters are professional theaters with a permanent staff, while most children's theaters are small and depend greatly on volunteers unless they are members of LORT.

The Jobs Theater Lovers Want

There's no business like show business for theater lovers. They want to work in the same world legends like the Barrymores,

Helen Hayes, Richard Burton, and Laurence Olivier once inhabited. Hollywood stars like Elizabeth Taylor, Matthew Broderick, and Nicole Kidman and television stars like Marie Osmond, Helen Hunt, and David Hyde Pierce have also felt this magical attraction. It is not just the stars that attract theater lovers; it is the magic of seeing plays such as *Death of a Salesman* and *A Streetcar Named Desire*. In the first days of theater, there really weren't any jobs for theater lovers: the playwright did everything, including acting. Over the years, more specialists emerged to help performers bring plays to life. What follows is a bird's-eye view of some jobs in the theater. In large companies there will be many jobs for assistants and interns, while in small companies individuals will handle several jobs.

Directors

Directors are the interpreters of plays. They make the decisions that determine what the production as a whole will be like. This involves working with the designers of scenery, lighting, and costumes before and during the rehearsals so that each aspect of the play will reflect the planned mood or theme. Another area of responsibility for directors is selecting a cast that will give the desired performance. Directors also supervise the rehearsals and coordinate the work of everyone involved in the play to create the final product.

Directors may have collaborators, including assistant directors, stage managers, and secretaries. The stage managers are normally in charge of organizing tryouts and of backstage activity during performances. The route to becoming a director can often be traced back to having been a secretary, an assistant director, or a stage manager. Another path is through an internship as an assistant director. Most directors have learned this craft through studying in a theater program in college and graduate school.

Career Advancement and Earnings

The first work of fledgling directors is typically done while they are in college and is unpaid. Then they will usually work as directors of small productions for which they will receive a fee. It is not until directors have a body of twenty to thirty works that they are hired full-time. At this point, they may receive salaries in the low twenties. Because so many theatrical companies are small and only have one director, advancement in this profession usually occurs by moving to ever-larger companies. A few top directors have become millionaires through their work as directors of highly successful Broadway productions.

Artistic Director/Managing Director

The Indianapolis Civic Theatre is one of the largest community theaters in the United States. It is professionally staffed and has a budget of more than $1 million a year. Robert J. Sorbera is the executive artistic director, which means he is artistic director as well as the managing director—usually two jobs. He is responsible for both the artistic and business sides of the theater. As artistic director, Bob has the important responsibility of establishing the artistic philosophy of the theater and overseeing the quality of the productions. A big part of his job is selecting the plays performed in the theater. In addition, Bob will usually direct three or four plays each year, which requires him to work at night five or six days a week during the six to ten weeks a play is in production. This job is very work intensive as, on the business side, Bob has the responsibility of overseeing operations, marketing, finance, development, and the education program.

Career Preparation

According to Bob, preparing to become a director is quite a complex undertaking. He believes that you need to have a certain amount of life experience in order to understand and handle the issues that you will be dealing with in plays. Also, because a director needs to be able to visualize what a play will look like, college course work in art and painting is important. In addition, there is the need to communicate your vision to set and lighting designers, which requires understanding not only the technical vocabulary but also what can be accomplished by these technicians. Since the 1950s, most directors have prepared for this career by studying how to direct in college. Bob earned a bachelor's degree in theater and his master's in directing. While in college, he directed a number of plays to qualify for his degree.

Career Path

Bob, like most college graduates who aspire to become directors, found it difficult to get his first directing job. He began by doing a play here and there for free or just a $50 fee. These jobs helped him build a resume and led to his becoming the artistic director at a small theater outside of Green Bay, Wisconsin. After two years, Bob moved to the San Francisco Bay area, where he freelanced as a director with a number of companies. His next career step was to become a technical director at a children's theater, where he really learned the mechanics of putting on a production from stage carpentry to sound to lighting. This enabled him to communicate effectively with technicians. After a short stint, again as a freelancer, Bob took a position as the artistic director of a community theater in Saginaw, Michigan. He remained there for eleven years before taking his current job at the Indianapolis Civic Theatre.

Career Advice

Bob describes directing as a highly competitive job where only the best survive. It is also a career that requires long hours that last far into the night. In addition, it takes years to earn good wages in this field. Nevertheless, Bob encourages those who love directing to persevere in becoming directors because each day of their careers will give them the artistic satisfaction they crave.

The Business Side of Theater

While most theater lovers may envision themselves working backstage, there are many jobs in the theater offices that must be done to keep a theater company functioning. Within this arena are the fund-raisers, accountants, box office staff, publicists, marketing experts, educational program coordinators, group sales managers, and the clerical staff. And when a theatrical production goes on tour, a tour manager is needed to handle transportation and living quarters, oversee publicity and the payroll, and deal with the presenters who are providing the facility for the play. In the commercial theater, a producer is needed to find the money for a play and hire the staff to produce it. Many theater lovers can enjoy a career within the business confines of the theatrical world.

Director of Marketing

The responsibilities of marketing directors will vary because of the different needs of theater companies. When James Habegger was director of marketing at the Indianapolis Civic Theatre, he was in charge of group sales, direct publicity, and advertising. He worked with a marketing team of four people to promote the theater with the public. They were the executive director of the theater, the director of marketing, the director of development, and the director of publicity. Teamwork was the key to his job. When James had a good radio or television spot and the director of development had a good corporate sponsor, they worked to bring these two elements together.

Career Path

James's college background is in performance arts and music. His interest in the theater can be traced back to high school and college performances in musicals. After graduation from college,

James pursued his musical interests by performing at Bear Creek Farms, a one hundred-seat theater, as part of a group that put on musical reviews. James's next job was at a dinner theater in North Carolina where he performed in five shows a week and made $35 a show. To earn living expenses, he worked as a maintenance man in a hotel. After a year in show business, James went to work with an insurance company because he simply couldn't make enough money in the theater. His job consisted of answering angry phone calls eight hours a day, which he feels was good training for working with the public as a director of marketing. James had just started taking marketing classes when he obtained his job at the Civic Theatre. At night, this theater lover would perform in musicals at another theater, since returning to his own theater would be like going back to work.

Director of Development

Directors of development are fund-raisers. Kathy Daniels raises money for the Civic Theatre from individuals, corporations, and governmental entities. Part of her job consists of cultivating an awareness with potential donors of what the Civic Theatre is, what it does, and how their donations will benefit the community and the theater.

Approximately half of Kathy's time on the job is devoted to securing and writing grants. Every year, she applies for more than twenty grants. She has to meet the deadline for each grant and fulfill the different requirements every grant has. A part-time assistant helps her accomplish this task. Another part of her job is developing brochures for the annual campaigns directed at individuals and corporations. Not only does she develop the brochures for these campaigns, she also creates the database of potential donors for these campaigns. In addition, Kathy has developed sponsorship packets that highlight the benefits of corporate sponsorship to the companies and to the community. The company logo is then in placed on all ads. To build ongoing relationships with the sponsors, she keeps them up-to-date with what is happening at the theater and gives them copies of press releases and ads and some free tickets. It is also necessary for her to keep track of all money that she is able to raise and to send acknowledgments to all donors thanking them for their gifts or sponsorships.

Job Requirements

Being a director of development at the Civic Theatre is a real hands-on job. Kathy answers her own phone calls and spends a lot of time on the computer typing and creating materials. While Kathy does not hold a degree in arts administration, which lets future development directors specialize in the areas of fundraising and public relations, she has taken many continuing education courses sponsored by the National Society for Fundraising Executives and courses at the Indiana University Center on Philantrophy. So far, she has taken courses on annual campaigns, planned giving, major gifts, capital campaigns, and grant writing and found them very helpful. To succeed in a job in development, Kathy believes that you must like people and be excited about and believe in the product you are selling, just as she believes in the productions and programs of the Civic Theatre. Then, it is much easier to ask people for money.

Volunteer Coordinator

Adrienne Reiswerg grew up in New York City, close to Broadway. She went to many shows with her family and developed a love of the theater when she was quite young. Adrienne has continued this family tradition by taking her sons to the theater in Indianapolis. In school, camp, and college, she was involved in dramatics. Adrienne's college training was in education, and she taught elementary school for five years. On returning to the work arena after starting a family, she obtained a job working for the

Riley Hospital Telethon as a volunteer coordinator. The job of recruiting volunteers and designing volunteer projects had flexible work hours, involved some travel, and gave her the opportunity to work with different groups. She left this job to enjoy raising her family, acting in community theater, and serving as a volunteer at the Civic Theatre.

While Adrienne was a volunteer, money became available at the Civic Theatre to hire a person to match interested volunteers with programs needing personnel, to expand the volunteer program, and to create new projects. The sum available for this position was only sufficient to fund a part-time job, which was ideal for Adrienne. For several years she worked nineteen hours a week as the volunteer coordinator, with some weekend and evening hours.

Adrienne got her job through her activities as a volunteer because she was in the right place at the right time and because she was able to accept part-time work. Prerequisites for this job include the ability to speak in public, write clearly, and organize and execute projects. In this field, you should also like to work with people. While a theater or college degree is not essential for her job, most theater companies tend to hire individuals with degrees.

Adrienne enjoyed her job because she worked with wonderful people, while making a contribution to the theater. She also found it satisfying to know that she was part of an organization that brings beauty and recreation to so many—in addition to being thought provoking. At the present time, the position of volunteer coordinator is extremely important to community theaters, since limited budgets are forcing them to turn to volunteers to do many jobs.

Because Adrienne was only a part-time employee, her benefits were not the same as those of full-time employees with health and insurance benefits. However, she enjoyed the benefits of flexible hours. And believe it or not this theater lover spent part of her free time doing volunteer work at other theaters.

The Technical Side of Theater

Costume Designer

Clare Gee became interested in theater during high school. Because her school was small, she became involved in every aspect of the theater when she participated in plays—from acting to set building. Bitten by the theater bug, she planned to major in English and minor in theater at college. However, after two years of college she changed her major to science and became a science teacher.

Working as a freelance seamstress gave Clare the opportunity to learn sewing techniques. Her introduction to the world of costume design came when she volunteered to sew for a theater. Through this activity, she learned costuming skills that she put to work with her theater background. Then she became a freelance costume designer, making costumes for local theaters. The next step was a position as costume supervisor at the Christian Repertory Theater, where she now works four or five hours a day and enjoys a flexible schedule. After making costumes for one show at the theater, she was asked to organize and operate the costume shop.

Clare uses her educational background, especially her history courses, when she is doing research to determine what type of costumes would be appropriate for a play. She especially enjoys the study and research and then moving on to a new and different project. She picked up her sewing skills through personal practice and has taken art courses to improve her sketching.

As Clare has demonstrated, it is not difficult to get into the costume design department at a community theater as a volunteer. However, to be paid for this work you must demonstrate that you are efficient, can be creative with the allotted budget, and produce good design work. In the future, she is considering a career in costume design in television or movies, which pays better than theater, but she is undecided about this. She still loves theater.

Set Designer

Sets aren't just pretty backgrounds for theatrical productions. They are the environment where the action takes place. Sets add to actors' characterizations as well. If the curtain goes up on a messy room with papers all over the floor, you get a different impression of the character who lives in this room than if the room were absolutely spotless. Sets also tell the audience about the time and place a play is portraying—such as colonial or Victorian, in New England or in Mexico. Audiences can also expect the set to define the mood of a play. Successful sets increase an audience's understanding of a play.

For several years, Joel Fontaine was resident set designer for American Repertory Company (ACT). This was an unusual job since most set designers are freelancers. Joel's work in designing the set for a play begins when he reads the play a couple of months before rehearsals for the play are to start. If he were freelancing, Joel would also visit the theater at this time so he could make his design fit the theater. After reading the play, the next step for set designers is a meeting with the director to discuss what the play means. Joel may bring pictures to this meeting to show what he thinks the look or the mood of the play is. If Joel and the director have worked together previously, the first meetings are smoother. At the next meeting with the director, Joel will have rough sketches or a model. The director's reaction can range from loving to hating Joel's initial ideas. However, over the course of three or more meetings with the director, Joel will refine his sketches until the two have agreed on a working model that is done to scale.

At this point, the producer of the play may also be consulted for his approval. Joel then makes a finished model—with every detail complete, from paint to furniture to molding on the door. A few designers have help from assistants in constructing the finished model. Joel then shows the director the completed model as a final step in the design process.

Joel did not draw the construction details when he worked at ACT. Instead, an ACT shop draftsperson would do this. While the set was being built at the ACT shop, Joel might check on it. Once a set was built, it went to the paint shop. At times, Joel had to give the scene painter a flat rendering of the set if the painting of the set was to be quite complex. During the time the set was being built, Joel had to confer with the lighting, prop, and costume designers. He wanted to make sure that all of these elements would blend with his design. He certainly didn't want an actor to be wearing a plaid outfit in the same design as the upholstery on the couch.

When he freelances, Joel may draw the construction details, paint the set, and get the props. Joel will go to a play rehearsal and show the actors the model of the set and will check at this time to ensure that the actors aren't walking through places on the stage that will be walls. Approximately a week to ten days before the play opens, the scenery is taken to the theater. Now is the time the set designer checks that everything works as it should. The lighting and sound designers now come to work on the set. Joel will be at the technical rehearsal while all the lighting and sound problems are solved. The actors wear their costumes at the dress rehearsal, and changes are still being made so everything works together—scenery, lighting, clothes, paint.

Joel began his career in New York City assisting other designers and doing design work himself, after completing a master's program in set design at Yale. Joel is a set designer in the theater simply because he can't imagine doing anything else. The two major frustrations of his career as a freelancer are low wages and always having to be looking for his next job.

Design Associate

At the ACT, Joel had a design associate, Dawn Swiderski, who also freelanced and did shows at other theaters. She did many of the tasks Joel would have to do when he freelanced. Because ACT's theater had been destroyed in the last serious San Francisco earthquake, Dawn would have to go out to measure the visiting stage ACT was using for a play before Joel began designing the set. When Joel completed the set design, she did the construction drawings for the scene shop. She then served as the liaison between the set designer and the shop. She also had to work closely with the scene painter. At all times, she had to make sure that everyone in the carpentry shop and paint shop had all needed information. Dawn was already familiar with set design before she came to the ACT, as she had assisted professional set designers when she was in college studying for her bachelor's degree in theater design and production. After college, she got a design internship at ACT and became an associate designer when her predecessor left.

After four years with ACT, Dawn left the theatrical realm for a career in films. Her first job was as a set designer for *James and the Giant Peach*. In film work, a set designer's job is primarily making working drawings and models.

Dawn has now become an assistant art director, which involves supervising the work of set designers. The next step up the ladder for her is to become the art director of a film. When Dawn is working on a movie, she works long twelve-hour days. She works through a union that sets a base price for her work, and then Dawn negotiates her own deals. Set designers are paid on an hourly basis, while assistant art directors are paid weekly.

Set Builder

After the designer and the director have agreed on the design of a set, the designer or an assistant makes a detailed set of drawings that shows every detail of the construction. Large theater organizations will have their own shops or use independent firms that specialize in building sets. In the case of nonprofessional companies, the set designer and a volunteer crew may do all the construction using the stage as their shop. ACT has its own shop which also builds sets for other stage shows in San Francisco and throughout the country.

Before Ed Raymond became the union representative for the stagehands union, he was the scene shop foreman of the ACT shop and the technical supervisor of the ACT company. As shop foreman, he supervised a core crew of four or five plus a scene painter. Depending on the time allotted for a job, the complexity of the set design, and the money available, Ed's crew could expand to as many as twenty people. Everyone working on the crew, including Ed, was a member of the union. When Ed needed to hire additional crew, he hired union people who could do the job. The union has an apprentice stagehand program to train stagehands for working in the theater, movies, and television. Apprentices gain experience by scene shop work, lectures, and reading material for self-study. In addition to the union crew, Ed usually had two interns just out of college, working for a very small amount of money to get exposure to set building and designing.

There was not much turnover in Ed's crew because they truly enjoyed this work. Job seekers who get crew jobs usually have had experience building scenery in college or elsewhere. It must be pointed out that these jobs, including Ed's, are seasonal. The crew only works when there is a job to do. For Ed, this usually meant approximately eight months a year. Only a few scene shops will employ crew full-time.

In his role as shop foreman, Ed often found himself covered with sawdust as he worked with his crew to build the set. They frequently had to consult the blueprints to make sure the set was being built precisely as the set designer envisioned. The designer consulted with Ed during the design process to ensure that design ideas could be built within the budget allowed and that the set as designed could be constructed as a light and portable unit. Ed's job as shop foreman included deciding which materials would be needed for each job and then ordering them. He also had to make sure that all of the work was done within the limits of the budget. In addition to building the set, Ed's crew was responsible for constructing all the mechanical effects—the elevators, cranes, and winches—used in a show.

When a set was built, Ed's job as technical supervisor began. In that capacity, he coordinated taking the set to the theater with what was actually happening at the theater. While at the theater, as well as in the shop, he worked directly under the production manager. He would stay on the set during rehearsal to make sure everything about the set was functioning as planned. When the production had finished its run, Ed was in charge of removing the set. Since each set is unique, few sets are stored. Instead, only the recyclable elements are saved.

Career Path

Ed never planned to work at building scenery, even though he possessed considerable skills developed from using the excellent shop in his family's home. He graduated from college with a degree in English literature and taught in elementary school, high school, and college for a while. Then a friend who was an assistant foreman in the shop at ACT told Ed about his work, and Ed was intrigued enough with the job description to start as a shop general, the lowest position in the shop. His job was basically to keep the shop clean.

Ed then became a shop mechanic. This is the job title for those who read the blueprints and assemble the sets. After a stint as assistant foreman, Ed changed his job milieu and went to work as an assistant stage carpenter. In this job, he was responsible for putting up the set when it was delivered to the theater. At this particular theater, he might have to put up the sets for two shows in one day. This was a full-time job with seventy-five- to eighty-hour weeks. During that time, he also toured with ACT as a property master in charge of the show's props. Then he returned to the ACT scene shop as foreman. When Ed was not working at ACT, he worked for a film company, Lucasarts, as a foreman and as a construction coordinator. This job was very similar to what he did at ACT except that the sets, crews, and budgets were bigger.

Lighting Designer

As a freelance lighting designer, Derek Duarte is in charge of all the lighting for a play or theatrical production. He must organize the technical elements as well as the artistic design. His job starts at the beginning of rehearsals and lasts to opening night, when an electrician takes over running the lights for the actual performances. By the time the curtain goes up on opening night, all the instructions for running the lights have been put in the computer.

Derek starts his work with four bare walls, a blank canvas on which to create all the lighting effects. For example, if the director says that a scene will take place on a stormy, hot night, Derek will have to create this night with the lighting designs he selects. Like the set and costume designers, he must read the play and meet with the director, as well as the other designers. Set designers and costume designers can make drawings or have fittings before the start of rehearsals, but it is a different story for lighting designers, who can make schematic drawings but cannot really put the finishing touches on their work until load-in time. This is the time when everything is brought to the theater and rehearsals on the stage begin. During this time, Derek will put in extended hours, working six days a week, from eight to midnight. Eighty percent of lighting designers' work is preproduction planning. The rest of their work is done after the scenery arrives.

Being a lighting designer is an exciting, high-pressure job, but Derek finds it fascinating each time he sees what he has created. Derek has been working in the lighting industry for the last twenty years.

Derek has known since he was sixteen years old that he wanted to work in the theater. He always knew that he did not want to be on the stage as a performer, so he looked through a theater program for all the jobs listed for a theatrical production; he decided that being a lighting designer was the job for him. After attending a community college, he got his bachelor's degree in dramatic arts from the University of California at

Berkeley. While he was at the community college, he participated in a work study program, getting minimum wage for being a stagehand. At college he worked at the renowned Berkeley Repertory Theater, a wonderful experience because the performers were from around the world. Derek obtained a master's degree in fine arts in lighting design from the University of California at Los Angeles. During his graduate studies, he was a teaching assistant and ran a lab on constructing scenery. All of Derek's jobs during his college days augmented his classroom instruction while paying for his schooling.

Career Path

After graduation, Derek took numerous small jobs in the performing arts. He really never lived anywhere, but instead traveled from job to job, living in New York, San Francisco, and Los Angeles. There is considerable travel involved in being a costume, set, or lighting designer, as you have to go to where the jobs are. Derek has even traveled to Hong Kong to do a show. Returning to the San Francisco Bay area, Derek took a job teaching lighting design for one year at Cal Berkeley, replacing someone on sabbatical. Since then he has kept the Bay Area as his home and worked for community theaters around the country. Today, besides being a lighting designer, he teaches theater crafts at the University of Santa Clara. In his free time, just like every other theater lover, Derek enjoys going to the theater; however, it usually takes him ten minutes to relax and settle in to enjoy the show. During those first ten minutes, he is busy checking out the set's scenery and lighting.

Sound Designer

Sound designers produce the program sound, which includes both sound effects and sound reinforcement. To make the ideal contribution to the production, the sound designer has to make the sound an integrated part of the production. Sound includes music, noises of no recognizable origin, realistic sounds such as doorbells and thunder, and any sound that is mechanically produced. In the theater, sounds that are produced electrically are considered to be part of the stage lighting.

The sound designer helps set the play's mood and enhance the story through sounds like gunshots, offstage screams, and screeching brakes. Sounds can either be live and created for each production or prerecorded. The sound designer holds the same type of discussions with the director as the costume, set, and light designers do, only this time the discussion is about what should be heard during the play. Sound designers will select sounds and play them to the director for approval. Once the sounds have been approved, the sound designer will make a list of the equipment to be used and where it is to be placed. Like the lighting director, much of the work will be done after the load-in. The sound director will also be concerned with enhancing the sound of the actors and the orchestra, if there is one.

Important Facts About Theater Jobs

Individuals considering a career working behind the scenes in the theater should realize that jobs in the performing arts are not usually permanent, except for jobs of an administrative or clerical nature. Jobs such as director and costume, set, and lighting designers usually begin and end with a show, unless one is working for a LORT theater. People take jobs in the theater because they love the surroundings. Many individuals working in the theater also hold outside jobs to earn more money because jobs in the theater do not offer high wages or job security. As you read earlier in the chapter, besides freelancing as a lighting designer, Derek Duarte is also teaching at a university. He tells his theater students that most of them will be working at another job but will find every moment they work in the theater a joy.

Searching for a Job in the Theater

Many people currently working in the theater found their first jobs after working as interns or volunteers with a theater. Networking is another way to find out about jobs. In addition, the following newspapers and periodicals have job information for theater lovers.

Newspapers

Shoot (weekly). 1515 Broadway, Twelfth Floor, New York, NY 10036

Billboard (weekly). 1515 Broadway, Eleventh Floor, New York, NY 10036

Variety (weekly). 5700 Wilshire Boulevard, Suite 120, Los Angeles, CA 90036-3659

Daily Variety. 5700 Wilshire Boulevard, Suite 120, Los Angeles, CA 90036-3659

Magazines

Theatre Design and Technology (quarterly). 330 West Forty-second Street, New York, NY 10036

Lighting Dimensions (seven issues per year). 31706 South Coast Highway, Suite 302, South Laguna, CA 92677

CHAPTER SIX

More Careers for Culture Lovers

Enjoying Other Fine Arts

"Culture, the acquainting ourselves with the best that has been known and said in the world, and thus with the history of the human spirit." MATTHEW ARNOLD, *Literature and Dogma*

W hen people speak of culture lovers, some may just think of people who love art, music, dance, and the theater. This is a rather narrow view, since the cultural world also includes literature, architecture, photography, furniture, textiles, and jewelry. As the list of arts and culture expands, so does the list of possible jobs for culture lovers. There are certainly jobs in museums, galleries, corporations, and stores for culture lovers with these interests. The list of possible jobs keeps increasing when you consider all the jobs that deal with more than one art form. Government agencies, foundations, and concert halls offer enticing opportunities for the culture lovers who want to work with several arts.

Be creative in searching for your perfect job in the arts. Investigate the possibilities by reading the want ads in your field of interest. Many of the culture lovers described in this book found their jobs in this way. Don't shun the lowest job on the career ladder in your field of interest, since it will acquaint you with the existence of more jobs in this area than you probably ever imagined. And remember that many of the culture lovers in this book found jobs by serving as interns or volunteers. Culture lovers should also search for jobs by such traditional routes as school placement offices; city, state, and federal employment offices; and private employment agencies. Here are just a few more places where art lovers can find jobs.

Unique Stores That Cater to Culture Lovers

There are stores that specialize in the selling of fine arts objects and very elegant objects for the home. Some of these stores are world famous, like Gump's in San Francisco. These stores do not just exist in metropolitan areas. Within many communities, there are stores that seem almost like museums—places in which to browse rather than to shop. They are intriguing places for culture lovers to work, especially if they are interested in several forms of arts. Culture lovers may find it especially appealing to work as salespersons and buyers in these stores.

Working at a Very Special Store

For many years, Ron Schwarz worked at Gump's, where his office was a culture lover's delight. Oriental scrolls hung on the walls, and sculpture abounded. Nevertheless, his desk was stacked with papers attesting to the fact that there was considerable paperwork in his jobs as divisional merchandise manager for the third floor and director of interior design. As part of these jobs, he bought all the lamps, furniture, and Asian art sold in the store. This involved seeing sales representatives in his office, going to shows and furniture markets, and traveling to such cities as New York, Paris, and Milan. These buying trips were not artistic flings, since he had a budget that limited what he could purchase. An important job requirement for buyers is to have a business sense. In addition, Ron points out that successful buyers must go beyond their personal tastes and choose items that would appeal to the commercial market.

Ron's jobs carried many responsibilities. He helped create the room settings on the third floor and supervised the look of the floor. He coordinated the colors used in the store. He supervised personnel and hired new sales associates and interior designers. For both of these positions, he was more inclined to look at a job seeker's background than at the individual's degrees. Because of the uniqueness of Gump's furnishings, clients from around the world seek the services of the design staff. Ron was required to spend time matching the clients to the appropriate designers.

Ron has both a background in art and experience in the retail and design worlds. Although he majored in art in college, he believes that his knowledge of the arts with which he deals comes mainly from constant reading, studying, looking, and visiting museums. Culture lovers aspiring to positions like Ron's with Gump's must have this attribute of always wanting to know more. In addition, they need to have a background of varied experiences.

Career Path

After the army, Ron's first job was designing a line of furniture for an importer, followed by a job working for an antique dealer, and then briefly owning his own interior design studio. A part-time Christmas sales job at Tiffany's led to a position as an assistant glass buyer in only six months and later to actually designing and buying china. In 1966, Ron opened his own store in San Francisco, where he sold such objects as china, glass, and silver and worked as an interior designer doing primarily residential work. After he closed his store to concentrate on interior design, he was asked to work at Gump's, which let him use all of his prior experiences. When Gump's discontinued the furniture and interior design departments after moving to a new location, Ron returned to his career as an interior designer. Today, he helps clients put together collections of antiques, which involves educating and consulting with them as well as finding fine arts objects for them. As Ron has clients throughout the United

States and the world seeking his expertise, his job involves considerable travel. It gives him an opportunity to shop throughout the world.

Antique Shops—Dealing in Valuable Art Objects

Many people tend to think of antiques as old household articles; however, other objects should be included in this category, such as coins, books, guns, toys, and even clothing. It isn't just age, however, that makes an object an antique. An object can be valued for the skill of its craftsman or because it is rare. Lovers of antiques can find jobs working with antiques as shop owners, salespersons, appraisers, auctioneers, restorers, and repairers. And there is no shortage of antique shops in which antique lovers can work. Large cities will have hundreds of shops, while even the smallest community may have a shop, especially if the area attracts tourists.

Owning an Antique Shop

For many antique lovers, a lifelong dream is to have their own antique shop to sell their favorite types of antiques. You will find shops specializing in oriental porcelains and accessories, seventeenth-century French furniture, nautical antiques, brass lamps, and whatever antique shop owners fancy. John Drum has owned his own antique shop specializing in eighteenth- and nineteenth-century decorative furniture for the past nineteen years. He has one salesperson. When hiring employees John looks for people who know the basic facts about antiques and are super salespeople. He believes that successful antique dealers not only must have an eye for what will sell but must also have good business skills.

John learned about antiques by growing up in a home furnished with eighteenth-century English and French furniture and other antiques his family had inherited. He studied marketing in college and worked in business for several years. After the death of his father, he decided to set up a very small antique shop with the possessions he had inherited. Before he opened the shop, he took a three-month course in London at the Study Center for the Decorative Arts. Subsequently, John learned about buying antiques when he went to Europe with a friend who taught him how to restock his shop. Today, he will make two trips to Europe a year, mostly to France. Over the years, he has established a network of shops to visit, but John is always trying to find new shops. Trip abroad are not restful. Days are often twelve to fourteen hours long and distances covered can be great. On one trip, he covered 3,000 kilometers in five days. He may just double park in front of a shop and run in and see if they have anything he is looking for. John also shops locally and attends auctions to restock his shop. Restocking an antique shop is a major job for every antique dealer.

Besides restocking his shop, John has many other tasks. He must spend time in his shop, selling antiques and seeing that the antiques he has purchased are repaired or restored if necessary. He will usually hire others to do repair and restoration work. Time must also be spent visiting other shops and studying catalogs in order to price his antiques appropriately. Before new articles can go on the sales floor, he must write up a description of the article for the sales tag and price the piece. In addition, like most other antique shop owners, he will take furniture to shows to sell it.

Books as Works of Art

In the middle ages, monks would sit at their desks in monasteries painstakingly copying books that were truly beautiful to behold. Today, there are calligraphers, papermakers, printmakers, typographers, bookbinders, and printers making books in artistic ways. These publishers often combine literature and art in a significant

manner. A few just print visual art with text. The material published by these companies do not have mass appeal. They are
rarely sold in bookstores, except rare and antiquarian stores.

There are no large publishers printing these books. Some are
just individuals with tabletop presses wishing to make outstanding books of a grandmother's poetry or a buddy's Vietnam War
experiences. Others are print shops with five or six employees.
Only a few fine print publishers make money; most are just self-
supporting.

Libraries and colleges often have book arts programs where
people can learn printing, typography, and other skills essential
to publishing. More information about this field can be obtained
from the Guild of Book Workers, 521 Fifth Avenue, New York,
NY 10175.

Publishing Companies

Book lovers can be actively involved in the publishing of literary
works at many publishing companies. Editors work closely with
the authors of fine literature in the preparation of the manu-
scripts of these books.

Antiquarian and Rare Bookstores

Book lovers do not have to print their own books to be associated with extraordinary books. A few bookstores just deal in
antiquarian and rare books, giving book lovers the opportunity
to own or work in a store buying or selling these books.

Performing Arts Centers

For the culture lovers who wish to be involved with opera companies, symphony orchestras, ballet companies, and theater and
choral groups, working as part of the staff at a performing arts
center provides this opportunity. The size of the hall greatly

determines the size and functions of the staff. The three largest performing arts centers are Lincoln Center in New York City, the Los Angeles Music Center, and the Kennedy Center in Washington, D.C. These centers have large permanent staffs with dozens of administrative and technical positions, as do many large universities with performing arts centers. Community performing arts centers, on the other hand, may be operated entirely by volunteers. However, these centers are excellent places for volunteers to get the experience that may lead to a full-time paid position with another center.

Staff Member at Clowes Hall

On the campus of Butler University, Clowes Hall is one place in Indianapolis where opera, ballet, musical, and theatrical productions are presented. While Clowes Hall is decidedly not as large as the three largest performing arts centers, it would be typical for a center this size to have a permanent staff including a general manager, business manager, development director, marketing director, public relations director, and operations director, plus all of the administrative and technical staff to support these positions. Anna Thompson is the education coordinator at Clowes Hall. In this job, she acts as liaison with the hall's resident opera and ballet companies and local educators. She also designs participatory workshops for teachers, based on the Kennedy Center model, and schedules matinee performances for schoolchildren. In addition, she arranges for preconcert lectures for the general audience. Whatever Anna does is designed to help audiences know more about the arts and the shows presented at Clowes.

Architectural Showplaces

There are places that have such interesting architecture that they literally take your breath away. It is a treat to stand in these buildings and view their design, the innovative use of materials, and the creative genius of the architect. If you visit such places as the Vanderbilt House in New York City, designed by George B. Post; Taliesen, the Wisconsin home of Frank Lloyd Wright; the Lincoln Memorial; or the Kennedy Center for Performing Arts, you have the opportunity to see architectural masterpieces. At the same time, there are opportunities for employment in these places that should be very appealing to those who are lovers of architecture and interior design. Employees are needed to handle the day-to-day operation of these places, which includes taking charge of administrative tasks from personnel to finance to public relations; operating gift shops; handling volunteers and docents; soliciting funds; renting the space for events; and running an education program. While some architectural landmarks may not have any paid employees, some have quite large staffs. Quite often, people who work in these places have first served as interns or volunteers.

Manager of Meetings and Events Marketing

One of the outstanding examples of modern architecture in California is the San Francisco Museum of Modern Art. It has a dramatic atrium space that is surrounded by four floors of galleries. Hillary Adams works within this magnificent setting as the manager of meetings and events marketing. It is Hillary's job to market the space of the museum to groups for parties and meetings and to ensure that each event held at the museum is a success. She finds it easy to market the space, as the museum is within easy walking distance of the convention center and major hotels. Instead of contacting individual corporations and conventions that might wish to use the space after the museum closes, she focuses on working with meeting planners at the visitors bureau and local destination management companies, as these organizations know who is looking for space for events. Hillary manages a staff of four people. Typically, a staff member will handle every aspect of an event, which includes signing contracts, filling out forms, arranging for tours of the museum, and working with the operations, security, and janitorial departments of the museum as well as the outside caterer. The staff member will also attend the event to be sure that everything runs smoothly. Quite often, this may become a true hands-on job as staff members may have to roll up their sleeves and arrange chairs, hang banners, or find an extra table at the last minute. Before Hillary got her present job, she was a staff member arranging events. She had also worked as a convention planner and in the development department of a children's science museum.

Job Prerequisites

To work as an event planner, Hillary says that you must be a very well-organized person who is capable of handling a lot of details but at the same time capable of seeing the big picture of what each event will be like. Because there are always surprises in setting up an event (the caterer may be late, you may have forgotten to order something), it is essential to be a flexible, can-do person who does not wilt under pressure. You also need to be someone who can work well with people from corporate executives to the cleanup crew.

Corporate Jobs for Arts Lovers

Many businesses have art, archives, and artifacts of historical importance that need to be preserved, organized, and shared with the public. Researching, managing, and displaying these resources are inviting jobs for culture lovers. The number of jobs in this area, while not large, may still be greater than you imagine. For example, the Wells Fargo Bank in California has thirty-five full- and part-time employees working in the history department of the bank. The bank's collection of art and artifacts dates back to the Gold Rush days in California and is displayed in bank museums in four separate locations in the state and in the corporate offices. Each museum has articles that are appropriate to that area's history and presents educational programs to schoolchildren. The most visible artifacts of the bank are the fourteen stagecoaches. They are seen in the museums, as well as in parades and civic events. Culture lovers working in this department of the bank even include stagecoach drivers. This department also manages the corporate archives that contain information about the development of the western frontier, since Wells Fargo is the oldest bank involved in financing in the West. Culture lovers who would like to work in this type of corporate setting should have backgrounds in art, history, or education. Beside having bachelor's degrees, several of the employees in this department have advanced degrees.

Corporate Giving Jobs

Watch a symphony or an opera on PBS, and quite often you will see the name of a corporation as the sponsor of the program. More and more corporations are associating their companies with the arts by sponsoring festivals, television programs, and touring companies. Some companies that are involved in giving to the arts have special giving departments. While there are a very limited number of jobs in this area, they are very appealing to culture lovers. Applicants with business experience are often corporations' first choices for these positions.

Jobs with the Government

In Europe, it has always been traditional for state and city governments to support the arts. Not until 1965 and the creation of the National Endowment for the Arts did the United States government really begin to contribute to the arts. The mission of the National Endowment for the Arts is

- to foster the excellence, diversity, and vitality of the arts in the United States; and

- to help broaden the availability and appreciation of such excellence, diversity, and vitality.

Culture lovers reading this mission statement can readily appreciate that within this independent agency of the federal government, there are many jobs for those who wish to be a part of implementing this mission. Block grants from the Endowment's program funds are allocated to state and regional art agencies, thereby creating additional jobs for culture lovers at lower levels. In addition, even the smallest communities now have local arts commissions that can be independent or supported by the state or local government. Culture lovers can also find jobs in museums from the Smithsonian to state museums, at arts centers like the Kennedy Center, and with a variety of cultural programs.

State Government Jobs

The individual states vary considerably in how they meet the artistic needs of their citizens. The decisions about which groups and individuals in each state will receive money to support their artistic endeavors are made by commissions appointed by the governors. The staff of the state art agencies, or councils as they may be called, usually makes recommendations to these commissions. Culture lovers with state agencies do such diverse jobs as develop arts festivals, work with the schools, help grant seekers complete their forms, and write informational books and pamphlets. The typical state art agency has an executive director, a fiscal officer, an information officer, programs directors, and a grants administrator, plus administrative and clerical support staff.

At the state level, job qualifications are very specific for each open position. For example, an applicant wishing to work as a music program director would have to have a background in music. Beyond having specific skills, applicants should have the following additional skills:

- a knowledge of accounting and budgeting so they can read and understand the agency's budget

- an understanding of the importance of teamwork

- the ability to work with volunteers

- experience working on cultural activities, such as festivals and art shows

Finding a Job at the State Level

Culture lovers wanting to find positions with the government in administering arts programs should visit their state employment office, which will have a list of current employment opportunities. You can also conduct an on-line search of your state government's Web site. In addition, in state and county capitols and city government offices, you will be able to pick up employment listings and view job openings on bulletin boards.

Salaries

Positions with state art agencies may or may not be civil service jobs. Entry-level positions usually pay college graduates in the low $20,000 range, while individuals who have top jobs like executive directors can expect to make between $35,000 and $50,000.

Federal Government Jobs

The procedure for getting a job with the federal government is complicated and often takes considerable time. The best way to understand this process is by reading a book like one of the following, which explain the steps you need to take.

Ronald L. Krannich and Caryl Rae Krannich. *Find a Federal Job Fast!* Woodbridge, VA: Impact Publications, 1998.

Rod W. Durgin, Editor in Chief. *Guide to Federal Technical, Trades and Labor Jobs.* Toledo, OH: Resource Directories, 1992.

David E. Waelde. *How to Get a Federal Job.* Fedhelp Publications, P.O. Box 15204, Department GOF, Washington, DC 20003, 1998.

Finding a Job at the Federal Level

The federal government has more than forty-four offices of personnel management (OPM) nationwide. When you visit an office, you will be able to view the list of job openings at the federal level and receive help with your job search. You can also phone or write the OPM for a list of job openings or find the list on the Internet at http://www.usajobs.opm.gov. Many government agencies have direct hire authority and will hire employees without ever listing their openings with the OPM. For this reason, it is important to initiate personal contact with the cultural agencies that interest you. It is often a good idea to write or call the department heads or supervisors and speak to them directly.

Two publications that can assist in your job search are *Federal Jobs Digest* and *Federal Career Opportunities*. The *Digest* is a biweekly newspaper that tracks federal vacancies and contains articles about job fairs, including those on college campuses.

Salaries

If you get an arts job with the federal government, you will probably be paid under the General Schedule (GS), which is composed of fifteen grades numbered GS-1 through GS-15. Each grade has a salary range of ten steps that is defined by the level of responsibility, type of work, and the various qualifications for each position. Employees are typically promoted through steps 1, 2, and 3 at the rate of one step per year. In steps 4, 5, and 6, they move up one step every two years. And in 7, 8, and 9, they move up one step every three years. This list shows 1998 salary figures.

Grades	Step 1	Step 10
1	$12,960	$16,214
2	$14.571	$18,335
3	$15,899	$20,669
4	$17,848	$23,203
5	$19,969	$25,963
6	$22,258	$28,936
7	$24,734	$32,150
8	$27,393	$35,610
9	$30,257	$39,338
10	$33,320	$43,319
11	$36,609	$47,589
12	$43,876	$57,043
13	$52,176	$67,827
14	$61,556	$80,151
15	$72,525	$94,287

Jobs with Foundations

The J. Paul Getty Trust is a foundation that operates five entities in the visual arts and related humanities, including the J. Paul

Getty Museum and the Getty Research Institute for the History of Art and the Humanities. Culture lovers interested in working for organizations that provide financial support to different arts groups can have gratifying careers working in foundations like the Getty Trust. Unfortunately, there is considerable competition for these jobs, and many are obtained by word of mouth or networking.

Foundations are incorporated nonprofit organizations that operate by giving grants to organizations, by operating their own programs, or by a combination of awarding grants and running their own programs. Foundations are established by individuals, families, and corporations who state the purpose of the organization in the by-laws. Some foundations are concerned solely with the arts, but many have broader interests. Small foundations may not have any paid staff or may be administered by a part-time director. Large foundations will have departmentalized staffs. The larger a foundation is, the better staff members are paid.

Culture lovers who are interested in working at a foundation should look at the *Foundation Directory* to determine which foundations support the arts, whether they employ a professional staff, and how large the staff is. This directory, published by the Foundation Center, can be found in public libraries and in the reference collections operated by the Foundation Center in New York City; San Francisco; Washington, D.C.; and Cleveland, Ohio. In addition, culture lovers should read the chapters on recruitment and career paths in *Working in Foundations,* also published by the Foundation Center, for helpful information on careers with foundations.

Volunteers and Interns in the Arts

A great number of culture lovers, just like you, dream of finding jobs related to art, music, dance, theater, and other fine arts. The competition for even entry-level positions can be fierce in certain areas. Imagine having to have a doctorate to get certain jobs at the Smithsonian. Furthermore, many positions, especially in museums, require successful applicants to have master's degrees.

Having the appropriate academic background is still not sufficient for many jobs that are extremely competitive. The edge to getting a job is often having experience, and two of the best ways to gain this experience are by serving as a volunteer or working as an intern. Volunteers and interns learn how arts organizations operate. They can discover interesting career possibilities they never knew existed. And they can perform so well in their jobs that they are offered positions where they have been volunteering or interning.

Careers for Culture Lovers

Working in careers in the arts raises the career satisfaction of culture lovers, because they are refreshed from working each day with the arts.

"The finest works of art are precious, among other reasons, because they make it possible for us to know, if only imperfectly and for a while, what it actually feels like to think subtly and feel nobly."
ALDOUS HUXLEY, *Ends and Means XII*

About the Authors

Marjorie Eberts and Margaret Gisler have been writing professionally for nineteen years. They are prolific freelance authors with more than sixty books in print, including twenty-one books on careers. The two authors have also written textbooks, beginning readers, study skills books for schoolchildren, and a college preparation handbook.

Besides writing books, the two authors have a syndicated education column, "Dear Teacher," which appears in newspapers throughout the country. Eberts and Gisler also give advice on educational issues in speeches, at workshops, and on the Internet.

Writing this book was a special pleasure for the authors as it gave them the opportunity to meet so many culture lovers who are bringing beauty into the lives of everyone who goes to symphonies, operas, ballets, museums, theatrical productions, and art galleries.

Eberts is a graduate of Stanford University, and Gisler is a graduate of Ball State and Butler Universities. Both received their specialist degrees in education from Butler University. The two authors also have more than twenty years of teaching experience between them.